I Will
Heal Their Land

Also by the same author:

GOD CAN DO IT HERE
SOMETHING'S HAPPENING

Available from Marshall Pickering

I Will Heal Their Land

The moving of God's Spirit in South Africa

Eileen Vincent

Marshall Pickering

Marshall Morgan & Scott
Marshall Pickering
3 Beggarwood Lane, Basingstoke, Hants, RG23 7LP, UK

First published 1986 by Marshall Morgan & Scott Publications Ltd
Part of the Marshall Pickering Holdings Group
A subsidiary of the Zondervan Corporation

British Library CIP Data

Vincent, Eileen
I will heal their land: God's work in
South Africa today.
1. Evangelistic work—South Africa
I. Title
269'.2'0968 BV3625.S.67

ISBN 0 551 01331 1

Typeset in Plantin by Brian Robinson, North Marston, Bucks
Printed in Great Britain by Anchor Brendon Ltd, Tiptree, Essex.

Acknowledgements

My grateful thanks are extended to all who gave me their time and assistance during my visits to South Africa. Many of their names feature in these pages, but especially I wish to mention Ed and Pal Roebert. I am indebted to them for their extravagant, loving hospitality in providing a home-base for me, between all my travels.

Contents

Preface

South Africa is in the forefront of world news. Commentators and politicians, like prophets of doom, forecast catastrophy. The political unrest hits the headlines; the whole world wants to know what South Africa is doing.

As repeated troubles shake the nation, thousands upon thousands of South Africans are praying. A different kind of shaking is taking place. The Holy Spirit has come with a new intensity of power convicting of sin, bringing thousands to salvation. God is at work in a whole new way. Never before has there been such rapid church growth; miracles abound with stories of God visiting his people with power.

The media only presents the bad news; this book seeks to proclaim the good news; true accounts of God's miracle working power, stories that never hit the headlines. My desire is that faith should arise; abounding faith which will bring the power of God into reality. I want to see signs, wonders, miracles and healing in the church, greater even than at its inception. These gifts haven't passed away – but our faith is lacking.

What God is doing in South Africa, regardless of instability and change, he is able to do anywhere. It is a testimony to the power of God that in such unfavourable circumstances the Spirit of God obtains mighty victories. Conflict rages in the heavenlies, shaking everything and bringing chaos; its impact is felt all over the world. Whose hand is shaking the nations? My eyes are upon him who shakes what can be shaken, and who plants, builds and establishes after he has uprooted, torn down and demolished.

May God use this book to stir up the church, give it a vision and a hope. The anointing of power will come upon those who earnestly seek him.

Introduction

Not only is there a wind of change sweeping over Africa, but in recent years the wind of God has been blowing over South Africa.

Things have taken place in the past six years that have not happened in three hundred years. All of a sudden, unusually large churches have begun to mushroom across the land. Only God could have done this! After centuries of 'small church' mentality, the Lord has supernaturally begun to break through this barrier. Today, large churches together with many related smaller churches are beginning to address our nation with a message of victory, faith and hope.

Not only is the New Testament five-fold ministry beginning to re-emerge, but a breakthrough into the miraculous is starting to be experienced.

It's thrilling to see the Antioch principle revived. These large churches are becoming mother churches with many branch churches emerging throughout the country. The growth has been so phenomenal that a mother church with its fifty to seventy branch churches have been recognised as a stream. Several of these streams have emerged in a matter of four to five years and together they touch the lives of some one hundred thousand people.

The most incredible thing that has taken place is that the three major streams have committed themselves to flow together. The identity of each flow, under the father-figure of its leader, continues to be recognised, but now they are flowing together under the single banner of the International Fellowship of Christian Churches.

Diagrammed, it looks as follows:

This coming together has obviously been a miracle of God. He told us to do it with the clear instruction that we must accept and declare the principle and subsequently he would assist us to work out the details. We declared it and now the details have been settled. As a result there is currently an enthusiasm and a unity amongst God's children that is almost touchable. The way has been prepared for God to command his blessing on South Africa.

Ed Roebert

1: Harvest Time in South Africa

As Sonna started to talk, the Holy Spirit said to me–'Listen, take note of what he is saying.' Sonna Mahabeer, a South African of Indian stock, went on to say, 'In our country God has planted some very large trees, their roots mingle under the ground.' As he spoke he demonstrated, entwining his fingers, then added, 'And in between the large trees are many small bushes.'

In the weeks that followed I had reason to reflect on those few words again and again. Travelling in South Africa I saw for myself how true a picture it is of the spirit of revival springing up in the country. Like big trees with huge trunks supporting weighty branches, certain men and organisations have an expanding and influential ministry to the whole land. Between them hundreds of small churches flourish in their shade.

My plane touched down at Jan Smuts International Airport, midway between Johannesburg and Pretoria, the capital of South Africa. Formalities were minimal. After brief greetings, Pal Roebert, a warm welcoming person showed me to the church office. The car slipped into an available parking space under spreading trees. As I stepped out, the cool breeze whipped my thin clothes. Pal grabbed her coat as we walked towards a low office complex, attractively arranged on three sides of a rectangle. Soon she introduced me to her husband Pastor Edmund Roebert in his small unpretentious office, the senior man in charge of Hatfield Baptist Church.

I had been looking forward to this moment. Although I

had never met Pastor Roebert, already I appreciated him. Kindly he made me feel at ease and sketched out in a few words the plans he had made for me. My intention was to experience what God is doing in South Africa. Some are calling it revival. Certainly there are plenty of compelling stories of miracles, healings, supernatural interventions and rapid church growth. Now I would have the opportunity to observe for myself and hopefully catch something of the infectious fire.

'I've arranged for you to visit Ray McCauley, there are thousands in his church and it's growing rapidly–you go and see for yourself. Yes, he's in Johannesburg, and so is Nicky van der Westhuizen. Now he is someone you must visit. At present they meet in a tent on the East Rand, at Roodepoort. And then on the western side of Johannesburg there's a place called Christian City with Theo Wolmarans, he's someone you must see too. And what about Durban–you should visit Fred Roberts. And did you know that Reinhard Bonnke is at present having a crusade in Cape Town?'

As I listened to Pastor Roebert I realised that God had planned for me a red carpet tour of his 'big trees'. I felt excited.

Hatfield Baptist Church

Hatfield Baptist Church was jolted out of its traditional mould through the sudden turbulence created by the 'charismatic movement'. Pastor Roebert received wisdom to harness the enthusiasm of those early days and consolidate a sound, growing church. Rising from his desk he said, 'Whilst you are here, Eileen, let's go into the church where you can sample a little of our history. Of course we do not meet here any longer, it isn't large enough.'

The attractive hall, with an extended area to create a large foyer, seated about 800 people. Pastor Roebert first joined

Hatfield Baptist Church in 1963 straight from college. The church then gathered in a small building, which has since succumbed to the bulldozers in favour of a new development. The church's next home was a disused cinema, and when they could no longer comfortably use that, they moved into the buildings where I was standing. It seemed apt that this pilgrim congregation, numbering approximately 2,200, now meets in a tent whilst waiting for a new permanent construction to be completed. Pastor Roebert, known as Ed to his friends, said that every move they had made into larger premises had meant growth. The step from the cinema to the church building seemed to invite a congregation that almost immediately filled it. After keeping fairly steady numbers for a while they made the move into the tent when about 800 new people came, and continued to come. Ed said, 'Whatever space is made available, will be filled.'

I stood looking at some Scripture plaques on the wall, 'Ask rain from the Lord in the season of the spring rain' (Zech. 10:1). Pal read it out. 'That verse of Scripture became a turning point,' Pal said. 'All these verses of Scripture hanging here are promises that the Lord gave us. Each one has had a significant effect upon our moving forward in faith. As a company of God's people we have claimed them and prayed them in, till we have seen God begin to bring his word to pass. Look at this promise over here, "From this day I will bless you" (Hag. 2:19). It seemed to flow automatically out of the first one. After Ed had preached on Zechariah 10:1, at the prayer meeting in the following week during a time of sharing, one person after another said the Lord had brought Haggai 2:19 to their attention. The word came alive to the people. On the following Sunday Ed preached on the same Scripture, "From this day I will bless you". The congregation stood and claimed the word of God in faith. We began to move into a totally new dimension of faith and expectancy. They were momentous days.'

Faith was soon rewarded, suddenly prayers were being answered. Many times that week Ed's phone rang, as excitedly people told him, 'Things are changing: God is beginning to move!' Ed preached on the same verse again the following Sunday. Like children the congregation stood a second time and claimed the same Scripture, 'From this day I will bless you'. Only God knows how many of those standing truly laid claim by faith to that verse of Scripture, but certainly Hatfield Baptist Church's history shows that from that time of response to God's word, blessing began.

Before those notable weeks in 1969, like many congregations hungry to see the power of God, they had spent times agonising before the Lord trying to search out every sin. Hours were spent praying, crying, fasting, yearning and longing, 'Oh God, come and meet us'. Now, standing in faith and believing the word of God, all that was past. It was as if sudden healing had come to a pain-racked body.

The new faith attitude among the people created a vibrant expectancy. They were on tiptoes waiting for God to move and ready to rejoice for every little blessing he showered upon them. Standing in that hall with the Scripture verses hanging about us, I felt built up in faith. These were no idle words, but the promises of God claimed by his people and brought into reality by faith.

All faith is tested, and testing is never pleasant. After about two months nothing very notable or sizeable had occurred. This became Satan's opportunity. One day someone said to Pastor Ed, 'Don't you think you're exaggerating this thing – "From this day on I will bless you"? We haven't really seen much, have we?' And so she continued to throw cold water on everything. The poisonous words, 'Has God said?' slipped down into Ed's heart and tried him. But he stood fast. No, God had begun to bless. He had fulfilled his word. Because Ed is an intensely honest man and no exaggerator, those carefully aimed darts searched out any corner in his heart where he wavered or doubted. He came through the trial the more confident; God continued, at first slowly, to bless and build the church.

We wandered out into the cool sunlight and drove to Ed and Pal's simple yet immaculate bungalow. In the garden every blade of grass grew in the right direction and I couldn't imagine that a weed had ever been seen! As we walked through the front door I could see Pal was a home-maker to her fingertips and an excellent hostess – her warmth and hospitality were shown in a dozen and one details. I met their three sons and was soon feeling like part of the family.

Although I had only been in South Africa a few hours I already had hundreds of impressions. Tingling with excitement, I knew I was going to see God at work in ways I had never seen before. A new sense of awe at the power of God's word had come into me. I found it surprising that reading hallowed promises could have made such an impression. As I went into the beautiful guest room I fell on my knees and thanked God.

My initial visit was for just four weeks, during which time I travelled extensively, sampling daily new aspects of God's work. Four short weeks, but they have changed my life! God is restoring power to the church to do the works of Jesus and to effectively preach the gospel. But the lasting personal impression upon my life has been a first hand experience of a supernatural anointing; a taste of a whole new dimension of life in the Spirit that God is restoring to the church. God is moving by his Spirit in South Africa. Those who are directly involved in the mighty things he is doing happily call it revival, although onlookers from less flourishing works usually qualify this.

Conscious that I had so little time and so much to see, once lunch was eaten, we went to look at the next phase in the development of Hatfield Baptist Church. As the church has now moved out from the district of Hatfield in Pretoria, it became necessary to change the name to one less specific,

Christian Community Centre, CCC for short. On a prime site of forty-six acres which was bought relatively cheaply when the area was undeveloped, the church is constructing a beautiful new complex with an auditorium to accommodate 4,500. We picked our way through the builders' muddle and walked up half-finished stairways from where it was possible to appreciate the overall design of the building due for completion in November 1986. The immaculate brickwork drew my attention. Each beige coloured brick seemed to have been laid by a master's hand with identical thicknesses of mortar between the layers. In detail as well as grand plan the building promised to be a fitting monument to faith, both for finance and in the promises of God. Around the new building the sloping land is rapidly being covered by new housing development, soon to become a new town.

Walking down from the building site we approached a large blue and white striped tent, the present Sunday meeting place for the church. We pulled back the flap and ducked inside. It looked beautiful – the sunshine giving an unusual lighting effect through the canvas. I enjoyed the warmth inside, but was assured it didn't feel nearly so comfortable in the cool evenings, when the sun had set. There was something of a permanent feel about the place with a carpeted floor, good lighting, large stage, beautiful flower arrangements and a bookstall. No wonder the tent had a permanent feel, they had been meeting there for two years!

Sunday Morning in the Tent

As a visiting observer I had the opportunity of appreciating the church's life exactly as it is, a privilege often denied to visiting speakers.

On Sunday morning as we drove into the car parking area, loving greetings were showered on us from every side. Pal was handed a tray of eggs, it seems she is supplied with all sorts of things from all manner of people. The church certainly love them. Today it wasn't the tent with its own particular beauty that grabbed my attention – it was the people. Crowds of them – filling the tent with life. Some of the congregation travel from long distances. I spoke to one couple who came from Johannesburg, forty miles away. They came because they enjoyed the particular expression of church life in CCC.

The church is organised so that the whole congregation can meet together on Sundays for celebration. All growing churches have to face the problem when space gets short – are they going to divide, or stay together? Ed made the decision – they would stay together for Sunday services for as long as feasible. It is part of their policy, Ed sees the necessity of one large church in the capital city of South Africa to stand like a sign declaring the power of God in the midst of divisions and traditionalism in the church and nation. The Christian Community Centre has begun to fill this need so that government representatives are not infrequent among their visitors.

From my position on the platform with the leaders of the church I surveyed the whole congregation. The majority were less demonstrative in worship than in many revived churches in England, although this didn't seem to inhibit the flow of the Holy Spirit. To my surprise, despite the size of the gathering there was a generous flow of the gifts of the Spirit from the whole body. A steady stream of people came to the microphone at the front of the meeting and brought prophecies, tongues and interpretation, and very accurate words of knowledge. One young lady got up from her place and spontaneously danced in the Spirit most beautifully, up and down the front aisle.

In the opening prayer of the meeting, the Holy Spirit was recognised as the source of their life, and a holy fear was expressed lest they failed to go the way of the Spirit, or through dullness of hearing, were left behind. The sense of reverent honouring of the Holy Spirit continued throughout the whole proceedings. The next few weeks were to present me with many opportunities of learning new ways of honouring the Spirit. Again and again I was impressed by sensitive openness to the Spirit. He was joyously worshipped and fearfully adored.

One simple method of honouring the Spirit is by giving thanks for what he does. On the Sunday before I arrived, through a word of knowledge, a twelve year old boy with crippled feet had come forward for prayer. He suffered pain and was incapable of participating in the normal school activities and sports events. Graham Jorgensen's feet turned over so badly that his shoes were permanently twisted. His father expressed his thanks for the healing in a praise item read before the notices, but Mr Jorgensen's joy spilled over into the evening service when he brought Graham on to the platform. The boy removed his shoes and socks and waggled his normal-looking feet in front of the congregation, then he said, 'The pain has gone.' Mr Jorgensen testified that the bones in Graham's feet had straightened out and now he had to wear new shoes to fit his new feet. Everyone shared the family's delight and erupted in praise and thanks to God.

The word of knowledge plays an important part in the ministry of healing. Whilst I watched, people from the congregation brought words of knowledge, some of them more exact and particular than I had ever heard before. The sick came forward, were prayed for and many testified to being immediately healed.

One enthusiastic couple told me they travel forty-five miles to come to this service. The wife, Rita Pittendrich, arrived at the meeting with a secret shared only by her husband and family doctor. That week a lump in her breast had been diagnosed. During the meeting someone came to the microphone and proceeded with the most accurate word of knowledge, 'There is someone here in this meeting, her name is Rita, and this week she has been diagnosed as having a lump in her breast.' Without hesitation Rita was out of her seat and was immediately healed. Bubbling with joy she told me about this miracle and went on to recount two others she had also received. Rita and her husband were thrilled about the church and what God had done for them, and thought travelling was a small thing in comparison to the blessings they had received.

As I made my way out of the tent after the meeting I spoke to two very ancient ladies who had been members of the church since 1927. Apparently a large number of the elderly, original members of the Baptist Church, are still with them. Casually I asked one of the ladies if it had been difficult to live through all the changes and upheaval in the church. Promptly she replied, 'Not nearly as difficult as the first twenty-six years, before Pastor Ed came and brought us some life!'

Points to Ponder

- *Do I have a progressive vision?*
- *Has God ever given me a promise or Scripture to claim by faith?*
- *Have I possessed it or let it slip?*
- *How can I honour the Holy Spirit in my personal life and do we corporately honour him in the church?*

2: Miracles in Cape Town

The decision was easy: I would go to Cape Town immediately. I didn't want to miss the last few days of the huge evangelistic campaign organised by Christ for all Nations. Pal returned me to Jan Smuts Airport only forty-eight hours after landing. Walking up and down waiting for the plane, I anticipated meeting another of God's powerful 'big trees'. Reinhard Bonnke, the German evangelist had already made the BBC news when he took the largest tent in the world into Soweto, the black township near Johannesburg. Now he had transported this vast canvas arena to the southernmost part of South Africa to begin his God-appointed commission to preach the gospel from Cape Town to Cairo. The brand new tent had been torn to shreds before the crusade began, but refusing to be deterred, they continued with the heavens as their canopy. I was anxious to be there and see what God was doing.

Briskly I walked out of Cape Town Airport, with its sterile, impersonal, hospital feel, into the bright sunshine. A transit van pulled up with CfaN written along the side, the logo for Christ for all Nations. I hopped inside and we headed for the freeway.

I took the opportunity to ask my questions about the tragic destruction of the tent, but the answers bouncing back were all so positive. 'Yes, the tent had been blown away, it was true, but . . .' and so I learned the first of a series of miracles that had been taking place in Cape Town.

In that southern part of South Africa June is a cold, wet, winter month. Humanly speaking, to conduct a crusade in the open air at such a time of year would be folly, yet God had intervened and made it all possible. In the most matter-of-fact fashion, Kobus DeLange, the operations manager, sitting at the wheel of the vehicle, said, 'On more than one occasion, I have driven through heavy rain along this freeway right up to the Valhala Park turn-off, the crusade site, where wonder of wonders, the sun would be shining. God is looking after us. Table Mountain would be shrouded in mist and we thought, "Surely rain must come," but day after day God has held back the rain.' For nineteen days he shone his approval upon them from a blue canopy above.

Rough Crusading

I arrived mid-morning when Suzette Hattingh was conducting a women's meeting. I sat at the back and watched the proceedings. About 5,000 women, mainly coloured, sat close together on the front benches of a massive area, extending way beyond the original boundary marked out by the tent. They listened intently to every word as Suzette powerfully preached the gospel. The crusade was beginning to have such an impact among the coloured population of Cape Town that many of these women had travelled in to Valhala Park from their townships outside the city on the train, early in the morning, with their husbands, when they went to work. With the mounting enthusiasm for the meetings they did not wish to miss a word. The meeting drew to a close and many women responded by going to the front for prayer.

The huge metal tent masts, at drunken angles, served as a reminder that there had been a tent covering the vast expanse of crude wooden benches. On one side of the seating area was a collection of portacabins, empty containers, caravans, transporters, arranged like an efficient little village – a veritable hive of activity. Two empty containers serve as dining rooms and others as a cook house, offices and maintenance depots. Many of the staff, including families with small children, live on site in the caravans. These mobile families dwell in permanent camping conditions whilst on a crusade.

I found my way to the office, housed in a narrow porta-cabin. Susanne, personal assistant to Reinhard Bonnke, was hemmed in behind a long table which served as a desk, around which there was virtually only standing room. At one end of the table someone was trying to receive a telephone call from Zimbabwe, whilst Betty at the other end, typed as fast as she could, endeavouring to replenish the stocks of labels for the ministry cassettes which were selling like hot cakes. Alongside Betty was a pile of coats, bags and valuables; anybody who needed to put something down in a safe place decided this was it. I settled myself into a corner and soon realised this busy group of people in the front line battle office hadn't much time for answering any questions.

The door opened and Reinhard eased himself past two men looking for cameras. Sitting down he started to talk as if he had all the time in the world although shortly, he was to address 50,000 people. What a relaxed, delightful person he is; every word and attitude bubbling with enthusiasm. His dynamic character relentlessly rises up like a fizzy drink in a glass! Immediately the conversation turned to the loss of the tent. In fighting form Reinhard dismissed the subject with, 'Oh, it's just Satan's lash-back, but God's got the victory.' It wasn't idle talk. Reinhard was in India at the time of the catastrophe, in the middle of an evangelistic campaign at Calcutta, where he had burned and trodden upon many Hindu fetishes. (How he enjoys trampling upon the devil's paraphernalia!) They were praising God for a breakthrough, many souls had been saved in that idolatrous city. The destruction of the tent was Satan's kick-back, but even before the 'phone rang to tell of the disaster, Reinhard was warned in his spirit by God, so the news broke upon him in small doses.

The conversation then turned to the uppermost thrill in

Pastor Bonnke's thoughts – the wonders God was accomplishing in Cape Town. Reinhard continued, 'We have had a fantastic response here each night. The lack of the tent hasn't hindered – why, it only seated 33,000 and we have had twice that number here in one meeting. Satan thought he was winning but God has blown our ceiling off!'

He chatted about his vision for Africa, 'For me to go from Cape Town to Cairo is not a difficult thing – it's just one step at a time. Country by country we will preach the gospel: Africa will be saved.' He oozed confidence. The vision was God's, the ability to accomplish it also belonged to God. At that moment I was very grateful to be in at the beginning; Cape Town to Cairo – by faith and without a tent. Jokingly he added, 'You will have to join us in Cairo when we arrive there.'

Mixing Miracles with the Mundane

I queued up and received a man-sized portion of mashed potato and stew, then sat on a bench at a long table with some of the workers. A group had just arrived in a light aircraft, part of the audio-visual team that would be taking aerial photographs for the publicity work. Sitting on my right was an exceptionally young-looking grandmother, Patsy Botha, a helper contemplating joining the team. Patsy began to tell me the most remarkable story.

Just one year previously she had been dying with TB. I was incredulous as I listened because she looked so fit and healthy – full of life. She had had major surgery where a large part of one lung had been removed, the other had mostly calcified. Patsy said, 'I couldn't walk more than eight or ten steps without panting and gasping for breath. I was desperately sick. The hospital sent me home, there was nothing more they could do for me – I had very little hope.' Everything changed one day with a visit from Reinhard Bonnke. She said, 'He wasn't in the home very long, but led me to Christ and simultaneously I was baptised in the Holy

Spirit. I didn't even ask for healing but was totally, completely and absolutely healed, look at me!' She bubbled over with joy.

As you can imagine after such an experience Patsy had a child-like faith for healing and went on to tell me another amazing miracle that had just taken place. The Sunday before I arrived she had a 'phone call from her sister-in-law Sheila, who lives in the Transkei. Sheila's sister Colleen, who is only twenty-seven years old, was dying of cancer. Patsy agreed to stand in the healing line at the crusade that day between five and five-thirty, when Sheila would pray. While Patsy stood as a proxy for Colleen, ill at Hendrina in the Transvaal, hundreds of miles away, God began to work. Colleen's body began to burn and feel warm all over. In the room where she lay in bed the television was switched off, but the face of Jesus appeared on the screen. She felt so well that she was able to get out of bed. Jubilant she telephoned her sister – she was healed.

Patsy was full of the most amazing stories. It seemed that miracles were part of her life, but with no more time she finished her tea and went back to the typewriter to meet the demand for cassette labels. As I walked away, I smiled to myself, 'What a strange place, the mundane and the miraculous are all mixed up together!'

On another occasion Patsy waltzed into the office triumphantly brandishing a fist full of pink decision cards; she had been to the post office to collect some mail. While on her errand, she prayed with six people and led them to Christ! Patsy has the most amazing knack of disarming people, talking of Christ and bringing them to decision. She is now in Harare, the capital of Zimbabwe, as a full-time staff member heading up the CfaN office.

In the camp-style washroom a black woman was walking up and down, praying at the top of her voice. She poured out her heart to God, pleading with him to save souls in the evening meeting. Another motherly old lady, one of the helpers in the cookhouse, grabbed me and gave me a hug and a big kiss, then proceeded with tears in her eyes to tell about the night when the tent blew away. 'Oh, Mama, we sat and wept like mothers whose babies had just died. You know those men in charge of the tent, they were like nursing mothers: up all hours of the night, pulling the ropes, releasing the stress, taking up the slack, they never left it, and then in the morning the wind got up and began to blow and blow. By breakfast time there were two big rips in the tent. Helplessly we stood and watched, the wind blew and blew, it didn't have any mercy. The tent made loud cracking noises, like explosions, as it ripped and tore, within half an hour the whole thing was in tatters. The dangling scraps of canvas looked like washing hanging on lines, everywhere we looked the site was littered with bits of canvas. What a day! It rained and rained, the wind blew for about six hours. I wasn't the only one crying – everyone was crying, even the men. It was like a funeral day. That was the sixth of May – before the crusade began.'

I returned to the office, opened the door and tried to edge my way inside. Hesitating for a moment I looked; had I come to a different place? The office had become a counting house. About ten people closely seated round the table, concentrated on counting a huge heap of coins almost running off the edge of the table. Nobody talked. Someone got up to leave, so I slipped into the vacant chair and had a crash course in recognising South African money. After each meeting this scene is re-enacted with every available pair of hands counting the offering. The mountain of money represented thousands of small gifts from thousands of poor black and coloured people. Among the faithful in this tedious task were Anni, Reinhard's wife, and their three children, who were at the crusade during their school holiday. About an hour and a quarter later backs were straightened and the mammoth task was finished.

After only a short time on site I was left with no illusions about CfaN's crusade ministry. If anyone is in doubt about the power of the grace of God he should go and see. It is by the grace of God that this diverse, committed group work together with such good humour. There is no glamour attached to driving a truck with supplies, working incredibly long hours, cooking and washing up in primitive camp conditions, manhandling the heavy, bulky equipment, securing the electrical supply fifty foot up a tent mast, or manning the tape copying machine for hours on end at the back of an empty container. Yet all these jobs and a thousand and one more are done day in and day out, joyfully, for the Lord. It is hardworking people like these who stand behind Reinhard Bonnke and make it possible for him to proclaim the gospel in such a mighty way to so many thousands.

The team is made up of many nationalities, blacks, whites and anything else; colour is of no importance. That in itself is a fantastic testimony in a country where colour and race are impassable barriers. Each person who joins CfaN comes with a call to co-operate in the evangelistic vision to see Africa saved. There are now about 180 workers, and however menial their task, their individual calling is of the utmost importance. The relationships between the different races, as I observed them, were heavenly. Warmth, love and friendship were openly expressed. Whether on the platform or helping out in manual tasks around the site, each person did his job without consciousness of race or position; hierarchy vanishes when everyone fulfils his own calling, honours his brothers and has a humble spirit. They were the kind of missionaries I loved, truly they had forsaken 'other things' and the 'delight of riches' to serve God.

Bearing the Burden

I threaded my way through the crowds jostling at the tables trying to buy CfaN T-shirts, and others milling round the bookstall. It was like an African market. I could see the prayer tent ahead – I wanted to observe for myself how they prayed. I felt convinced that secrets could be learnt from their praying, which would show me why the demonstration of God's power was so obvious in all their meetings. Pulling back the flap I walked inside the prayer tent. The change of atmosphere was stark – the niceties of life no longer covered spiritual realities. Sin, sickness and demons were blatant – just a canvas-thickness away, crowds in carefree holiday mood, laughed, shouted, shared jokes and food.

There was no furniture inside the tent at all. As I surveyed the scene, I realised there were three categories of people present; the pray-ers, the desperate and needy, and pastors and counsellors endeavouring to help them. I had only stood inside the tent a few moments when one of the African pastors guided me to a weeping woman, backslidden and deep in sin. She wept and wept her way back to God. I was a spectator to what God was doing in her life. I hugged her and we cried together as she poured out her confession to God. The canvas wall enclosed a haven where God worked powerfully.

I turned away, only to be confronted with another woman pleading with me to pray for her. She wanted to receive the baptism in the Holy Spirit. I laid my hands upon her, immediately she fell down as the power of the Spirit came upon her. For some reason I wasn't surprised, although it had never happened before. The power of God was so present in the tent. Gently I laid her on the grass and left her lost in God, her face aglow with glory. Nearby a young man lay floundering on the ground, his face contorted by evil spirits. It seemed as if heaven and hell met in the tent. While I watched the spirits being cast out, someone tugged me from behind. Uncontrollable tears rolled down my face as I looked at a most beautiful Indian child. He had no eyes. The young man with him explained. The boy, about nine years old, had cancer in both eyes and in an attempt to save his life both had been removed. Simply he asked, 'Will you please pray for him?'

Outside the people began to find their places on the

benches in time for the evening meeting. Songs of victory and praise sounded out from the musicians. Those in the tent for counselling and prayer now left and Suzette called the intercessors together. She came with an anointing upon her as if she had just walked out from the presence of God. With authority she shared what he had shown her – the manner in which we were to pray. 'Tonight God is going to heal.' Compassionately she spoke of bearing the burden of the people's need for healing and deliverance. As she spoke, I felt myself carried into a spirit of compassion, it began to permeate my emotions and I remembered Jesus when he looked upon the multitude and saw them harassed and helpless, like sheep without a shepherd. I could feel how he yearned for them – carrying them in his heart; I began to understand a little of what it is to bear a burden.

Suzette graphically shared the Scriptures to guide the intercessors how to pray. 'And it shall come to pass in that day, that his burden shall be taken away from off thy shoulder, and his yoke from off thy neck, and the yoke shall be destroyed because of the anointing' (Isa. 10:27 KJV). Carefully Suzette taught how the burden of the people must be received by the intercessors; it must come upon their shoulders, so giving the pray-ers God's attitude to the people's need. It is the way intercessors share God's heart toward the needy, another aspect of entering into the sufferings of Christ. By co-operating with the Holy Spirit as he prays through us, the burden is carried back to the Lord. Suzette showed how intercession is the work of burden-bearing in harmony with the Holy Spirit; truly the intercessor is a co-worker with God. By deliberately aligning our spirit with the Spirit of God, we become channels through which anointed prayer can flow. Worship is the oil that activates our spirit bringing it into harmony with God's purpose and sensitive to his whispers.

Praying, if it is going to be fruitful, must be an activity of faith. Suzette exhorted us to exercise faith for the anointing of the Holy Spirit upon our prayers. She cautioned sensitivity to the Spirit and not to attempt to come against the powers of darkness opposing the people, until we had prayed through the burden in our hearts. There is a place in prayer when you know God has heard and you know the anointing of the Holy Spirit is setting the captives free. 'The yoke shall be destroyed because of the anointing' (Isa. 10:27 KJV).

Using a megaphone to compete with the noise outside, Suzette taught in a workmanlike fashion; it could have been instructions for putting up the tent – she was so matter-of-fact. If you follow these steps, the devil will be defeated, the sick healed and souls saved. I realised in those few moments standing there, with about fifty intercessors, God had given me a new revelation of the power of prayer. What a mighty tool it is for the accomplishment of God's purposes! The little band of intercessors were charged not to be distracted from their prime task – praying. Suzette said, 'If the demon-possessed or others come seeking prayer one or two deal with them, be on your guard, do not let any tactics of the evil one divert you from the ministry of prayer.' With one last look at the young boy with no eyes, I went to pray.

The prayer tent was quite large, the small group of mighty intercessors were soon scattered and alone with God. Some walked up and down briskly, praying out loud and waving their hands about. Others were flat on their faces, weeping before the Lord. One elderly man stood by a tent pole, pleading and weeping, calling upon God for his mercy and deliverance. He didn't move from that spot the whole time. A vigorous young African walked up and down in the corner of the tent, talking to God in such an intimate fashion; I could see he was no stranger to the courts of heaven. He knew how to pray, just listening to him was instruction. With authority he commanded the demons to go, to leave the people and set the captives free. There was nothing polished or professional about the pray-ers, they are not 'white-collar' workers, but God's labourers; men and women prepared to get their hands dirty in warfare to accomplish the task.

Lifting the tent flap I slipped out leaving them to pray until Reinhard finished preaching. I wanted to see the results. From the platform I had a favoured view of the vast crowd. Like grotesque arms, the tent poles stretched up into the African night, carrying powerful lights which beamed out showing the parameters of the crowd, but the message was taken far beyond them by the powerful loud-speakers reaching into homes even a mile away. In the gloom behind the preaching platform I could make out hundreds of shadowy figures leaning on cars in the car park listening to the gospel.

The time had come for Reinhard Bonnke, the evangelist, to preach. He stood up, emanating vibrant enthusiasm. With a microphone in one hand, striding up and down the platform with fantastic vigour, he encouraged the people to praise God. From the word go, he was anointed. I don't think anything could have deterred him. Lifting up his melodious voice, he sang, 'What a mighty God we serve', and 50,000 people joined in. Faith rose, and he began to preach – the eager, expectant people hanging on every word.

As far as my eye could see there were rows and rows of African faces intently watching Reinhard's every movement. The majority were Cape coloureds with a scattering of white people and other black tribes. The overweight women, with woolly hats pulled down over their ears sat, ungainly, on the benches. Children were tucked in every corner, some sleeping on the ground. The men folk, many dressed in their Sunday best, were not so numerous, but like everyone else they listened with rapt attention.

Even as Reinhard began to make the invitation, people started to move forward. Hundreds streamed out of their places for salvation. Soon the area at the front was crammed, the aisles were jammed with people, benches were being removed – and yet the people kept on coming. Many openly wept, others shouted calling upon God. Something was happening outside of the normal experience of life – it seemed unreal, the people were beside themselves, I was sure they couldn't understand their own response. The unseen activity of the Holy Spirit drove the most hardened sinners to repentance, brought people running from their seats and reaped about 5,000 people into the kingdom of God.

Every effort was made to somehow counsel and pray with the hundreds of enquirers. Teams of trained counsellors stood in long rows as the enquirers filed past. Soon little knots of people were filling in cards and praying together. I only went to observe how this important task was to be accomplished, but immediately I was pressed into service helping the illiterate to fill in their names and addresses and praying with new believers.

. . . And Triumphs Through Prayer

I returned to the platform as preparations to call the sick forward were completed. Soon the first rows were pressed hard up against the platform as thousands of sick people pushed in closer. There were the most heart-rending cases amongst them; some looked as if they had never left their rooms or hospital beds for years – they were desperately ill people. The burden of prayer was still heavy upon my heart as I walked up and down on the platform, gazing at this incredible crowd of people, tears streaming down my face. I couldn't stop crying. The misery and human suffering spread out before us was heartbreaking. The blind, the deaf, the demon-possessed, the tragically deformed and the dying came or were carried by valiant helpers, pushing their way through the crowd with one hope – to be healed. I thought of Bible days – this must have been how the crowds pressed in on Jesus. He must have looked out upon similar clamour and confusion when his heart was moved with compassion.

Pastor Kolisang came to the microphone and with great authority spoke deliverance to those who were possessed of demons. Hundreds raised their hands seeking God to set them free. With shrieks and yells the demons went. Some people fell down – workers scrambled among the arms and legs trying to rescue them. The demons quickly responded to Pastor Kolisang's command to 'get out!' They knew him and recognised his authority. There was no sophistication about this crowd. The crush was so tight that little children were being pulled up on shoulders so that they could breathe and workers could barely squeeze between the bodies to rescue those in need. A thin woman in a trance, under the control of evil spirits, was passed like a pole across the heads of the crowd and dragged on to the platform. As the demons were cast out, she was transformed before our eyes. The yelling and screaming of demons gave way to shouts of joy and a trickle of people clambered up on to the platform to give testimony to their deliverance. Pastor Kolisang, such a tender, compassionate man, continued to pray for the sick. The heads of the people were about level with the platform, so he got down on his knees and reached out as far as he could, to lay his hands on the heads of those who pushed up close.

He began to pray for the blind and in the crush before me, raised up on a man's shoulders was the little boy I had seen earlier. I cried to God to fill his empty eye sockets. I wish I could say I had seen him healed. Nearby an old blind man raised his white stick calling on God. Prayers for the sick continued for about an hour encouraged by a steady stream of joyful people eagerly telling of their healings. Dancing for joy, people left their crutches and leg braces.

A woman still wearing a surgical collar walked steadily alongside her husband who pushed her folded wheelchair. Idly watching in the shadows was a man with crutches resting his weight against a parked van. 'Wouldn't you like to have been prayed for tonight?' I asked. Leisurely taking a cigarette from his pocket he lit it, and answered, 'I'm not sure about that sort of thing.' As he hung back in the shadows songs of victory were being sung, testimonies declared and two brave souls walked up and down the platform carrying their crutches high, thanking God for their healing. Praise God! Such wonders to be seen. Whilst that unbelieving man looked on, hundreds were shouting, dancing and glorifying God.

Suzette, the leader of the intercessors, stood, praying, still carrying her burden before the Lord. Victories won in prayer that night forced the devil to yield up captives; bondages and sicknesses had been broken, but it wasn't the end of the story. The following morning, when Suzette stood up at the women's gathering, she was unable to preach because God loosed a mighty power to heal and hundreds were set free in glorious manifestations. Prayer prevailed – Satan had to yield.

Reinhard said, 'I believe in the power of prayer. We have seen a fantastic increase since we set apart the intercessors for their ministry. God spoke to me, "CfaN needs prayer".' Suzette said, 'Reinhard is like the light bulb – he gives the light – the intercessors are like the power-house; unseen, working to produce the power for the light!'

Prayer on Scraps of Paper

The next afternoon I joined Betty and another woman standing at the back of a pick-up truck. 'We're sorting out prayer requests,' they said. 'Place those written in other languages here.' I put my hand into the very large box, took out a note and read, 'Please pray for my father, he is sick and can no longer work. My mother has six children.' The messages had been written on any available scrap of paper – some folded, others carefully addressed to Pastor Bonnke and put into envelopes – but all of them painted a picture of human misery. Betty said, 'As we read we are praying.' I took another, 'My husband is not saved and he drinks.' And another, 'My husband drinks too much and breaks up the house, please pray.' Dozens were desperate cries from women for unsaved menfolk and children. Those with too many children to care for, hopeless and without husbands, shared their plight. The box was full – hundreds and hundreds of prayer requests. Suddenly I was tempted to consider the whole activity futile. Was this prayer? Did these scraps of paper asking for prayers mean anything? Could my few words change the situation? Deliberately squashing the thought, I prayed more fervently. I would believe God answers prayer, even a whispered sigh as the unfolded paper dropped into the box. The back of the truck became a temple of prayer.

'Please help!' Anguish, misery, pain, heartaches, were all expressed in cryptic words. Some wanted to be saved, many needed work or deliverance; conviction of sin weighed heavily, forcing confessions. 'Please pray for me, I have murdered my seven-month-old baby.'

As we stood praying, crowds were streaming into the crusade site to find seats for the evening meeting. I looked at them with new eyes – the prayer requests had exposed an intimate peep into the misery of many of their lives. Turning back to the endless pile of requests, I wept. Thankfully I knew God heard our prayers.

Later, when I returned a second time to Cape Town, the Lord encouraged my faith by letting me know of an answer to one of those prayer requests. 'Please pray that my husband will come back home, he left two years ago, I have no idea where he is.' A woman had put that request into the box at the crusade on Friday night. The following Monday her husband 'phoned and was on his way home!

Holy Spirit Night

There was a chill in the gathering darkness but a warm anticipation in our hearts. Tonight was Holy Spirit night when Reinhard would call the people forward to receive the baptism in the Holy Spirit. Simple teaching on the baptism in the Holy Spirit is the focal point one evening in each of his crusades. Afterwards, on many occasions, the power of God has come down with such force that people have fallen to the ground altogether, like cut grain when the sickle passes through it.

As Reinhard preached, the Holy Spirit brooded over the meeting. Expectancy and faith was etched on every expression. The crowd seemed larger than ever, estimated by the tentmaster to be about 60,000 people. I noticed two white teenage girls working their way from the back to the front when they judged the end of the preaching was close. Bobbing between the rows, they carefully planned their strategy so as to be near when the call was given. They didn't want to miss what God was going to do.

We were about to see a miraculous outpouring of the Holy Spirit but first of all, in the same down-to-earth manner that I had encountered before, very practical arrangements were made.

A team of outstanding men and women surrounded Reinhard Bonnke. Those with expertise in organising massive crowds were certainly tried that evening. Sensing that the area in front was going to be too small for all those who would want to respond, benches were quickly removed. 'If you intend coming forward, first give your watches, purses, handbags, Bibles and all other valuables to a friend or relative before moving. They might get lost in the crush. Men come one side and women on the other.' The instructions rang out from the loudspeakers. It seemed an eternity before all the preparations were made. 'If the Spirit should cause you to fall down, relax, co-operate with the Spirit, let him do his work in your life.'

Except God had been in control that evening a tragedy could not have been avoided. Once the call was given, thousands of people surged forward at once. The crowd was so dense that I think they could barely breathe. The workers cautioned the people not to crush those at the front. There was another delay as the people were instructed to shuffle backwards. It seemed a strange atmosphere in which God would come and work. Surely the people would have to reach out in cold faith.

Reinhard lifted up his voice like a trumpet and began to pray. With their hands raised the people reached out to God, calling upon him to pour down his Spirit. Suddenly, with a huge crescendo of praise and a deafening shout of 'Hallelujah!' – the Spirit of God fell upon them. Some fell to the ground, but the majority wedged in so tightly, with hardly room to breathe, remained standing. Mixing their yells with the ecstasy of the Spirit were the demon possessed. As people came seeking God the evil spirits were forced out into the open and couldn't keep quiet. Many were delivered as the workers, with difficulty, pulled them from the crowd. Probably about 5,000 people received the baptism in the Holy Spirit at they stood crushed in front of the benches that night. Their exuberance knew no bounds. Shouting, praising God, laughing, crying, speaking in tongues – the sheer delight of experiencing God was written upon thousands of faces. It looked like chaos, but God was there doing amazing works in individual lives.

Long after the benches had emptied, thousands continued standing there, not wanting to leave the tiny patch of hallowed ground where God had met them.

3: Cape Town Revisited

It is so easy to get caught up in the whirlwind of excitement at evangelistic crusades when in reality the lasting results are only revealed by the number of new believers actually added to the churches. Long after the benches had been stacked away and the final tent mast pulled from the ground like a massive tooth extraction, I returned to Cape Town to see what had happened to the thousands of enquirers. During the eighteen glorious days of crusade 808,000 people had attended the meetings and 29,084 registered first decisions for Christ, including many Muslims.

A group of coloured pastors who had been involved in the pre-planning of the crusade eagerly talked with me in glowing terms of what God had done. They were a biased bunch, like Pastor de Beer, who said, 'Nowhere in the world could you beat what happened here!' And he meant it!

They had good reason to be thrilled, God had moved among them in ways far exceeding their wildest dreams. Before the crusade began 300 pastors came together in Cape Town, committing themselves and their churches to work co-operatively for the crusade. 'Surely it must be revival for that to happen,' said Pastor de Beer, and he went on, 'The response was fantastic.' And then all talking at once, they told of the escapades experienced in getting their people to the meetings. The Christians begged and bullied friends and relatives and brought them like trophies to the bus. Daily more and more people came – but the buses hadn't elastic sides, there was never enough room. Sometimes the buses broke down, sagging under the weight of 150 people packed into an eighty-seater bus. Arriving at the meeting was certainly an accomplishment, but the task wasn't completed until the whole operation was reversed and the people were home again. Many times it was after two a.m. before the pastor was able to flop on to his bed.

The wife of one of the pastors then spoke up. 'Never before have we seen people so eagerly running to meetings. I think it happened because of the intercessors. They did an invaluable job almost round the clock, calling on God to pour out his Spirit during those days.' All the heads nodded in agreement.

Pastor de Beer chipped in again. 'I can't get over the love and unity among the pastors. There hasn't been any competition; we've worked together in a brand new way. This is why God has blessed us.' 'For years we have been preaching the gospel, trying to build the churches – suddenly all is changed. It has been a miracle,' said Pastor Valentine, a leading Pentecostal.

'It began with the miracle of the weather. Local people advised the team not to come in the rainy season, but they felt from the Lord that June was the right month. They were tested, because even while they were erecting the tent it rained. I do not think the material could have been very strong as tears had to be repaired as the work went on. When the tent was finally pitched, before the crusade opened, a strong wind got up, a regular phenomenon in this Cape; it registered eighty-four kilometres per hour but could have been worse. Then the news came, "The tent's gone!" Like a burst balloon it was in shreds. I drove straight to the site. As I got out of my car the loud, violent, cracking noise of the wind whipping through the remaining canvas and stays was frightening. The huge concrete piles heaved in the ground with the tug of the wind. Everywhere I looked people were crying; it was like a funeral. Then I couldn't stop weeping myself. I wept and wept. That same day Reinhard, trampling upon fetishes in India, celebrated his anniversary of twenty-five years in the ministry.'

Pastor Valentine was full of emotion as he remembered that dreadful time. He went on, 'Of course we went to pray and God spoke to us in prophecy. "My glory shall be the canopy that covers the people and the praises of my people shall be the pillars."' Sitting on the edge of his chair and leaning forward, Pastor Valentine raised his voice ready to preach to a thousand – he was so excited. 'God certainly fulfilled his word – it was better than any tent! Each day during the whole crusade we rejoiced in a miracle – sunshine, blue skies and no rain – after the first day when we were tested!'

Growing Churches

The crusade doubled many churches, one had a 400 per cent increase and all are bulging with hundreds of converts. Now a second wave of converts – those drawn to Christ by the witness of the new believers continues to stir their enthusiasm for evangelism. 'We are thrilled; surely this is revival,' said Pastor Valentine. 'God has come and done something among us, we have fantastic unity. Everyone is co-operating to build the amazing harvest of souls into the churches.'

Valhala Park sports field, the crusade site, is in a Muslim area with a bad reputation for violence and crime, yet during the crusade all was quiet with no extra police presence – the whole time was peaceful. Pastor Mannas had ninety converts added to his church of about 150 in the Valhala Park district. Excitedly he said, 'The "Jesus fever" continues, many bound in witchcraft have been set free; they are so liberated it provokes more to come.' With the bold witness of converted Muslims, the challenge of Christ is not going away. A new chapter of miracles is being written since the crusade finished. 'We have seen a man healed from severe heart disease; a very wealthy Muslim woman accepted Christ and another Muslim couple came seeking God's blessing upon their pilgrimage to Mecca!

They were led to Christ and said, "We're not going to Mecca now, we're going to Jerusalem!"'–echoing a song often sung at the crusade. Healings, deliverances, miracles and salvation continue daily. God is at work in a sovereign way, bringing people to repentance. The churches have been pushed into a new gear and expect the pace to accelerate.

Behind the scenes there are always faithful men and women doing routine work: typing follow-up letters, collating the mass of information gleaned by the counsellors and passing it on to the churches. The follow-up office buzzed with people, telephones and typewriters. A coloured pastor walked in and stood awkwardly, with tears in his eyes asking for forgiveness because he had not co-operated during the crusade. He said, 'Last Sunday I had 150 new converts in my church. Look what God has done, and I didn't do anything to help. I am sorry.' In future he didn't intend missing out; quickly he offered support for coming crusades and planned to pray with the pastors. Without a doubt their zeal for evangelism would soon rub off on him. Taking a handful of follow-up sheets he left–there was work to be done.

Six months later I was back again visiting Cape Town. In the crowd outside the stadium where a follow-up crusade was being held, I bumped into Pastor Mannas. Still full of enthusiasm, he lost no time telling me of the continuing wonders God was doing for them. His church is growing, with a third wave of converts being added. I asked how many from the crusade had continued with the Lord. 'More than fifty per cent,' he said. 'Even though we lost some, our numbers are no less, so many more have been converted.' It was good news.

Very easily we can be ruled by statistics, head-counting and totting up–the world's methods of deciding whether a crusade was worth the effort and finance in terms of numbers saved. Somehow I have a feeling, God doesn't look at it quite in that way.

Suzette Hattingh took these questions to God. 'What about the enquirers, Lord, who fail to be added to the churches? And those who stray because the churches are inadequate to care for new converts or have no love for souls? Lord, look at the financial cost and labour in staging the crusade.' She questioned the economics of such methods. Then God spoke. Can you fix a price on a soul? If only one was saved would it be worth it? Suzette knew with understanding the price Jesus had paid for her salvation – could she set a lower price on others? Yes Lord, even for one. Never again did she question, only prayed more fervently for the churches and all involved in follow-up.

Praise God it is not only one, but thousands being saved and added to churches. Reinhard Bonnke, this mighty man of faith says, 'The day of the sickle has passed – it is the day of the combine harvester! God wants to do great things. Hallelujah!'

The Vision will be Accomplished

But what about the CfaN crusade from Cape Town to Cairo, now the tent has gone? First of all, the tent, the biggest in the world, a phenomenal undertaking, wasn't a man's idea it was God's. God owned the project, he initiated it, gave words of encouragement and promises through prophecies and then, glory to God – paid his own bills! Reinhard said, 'God pays for what he orders! If God has spoken, his word cannot fail to be fulfilled.' Reinhard said, 'Some of the promises given to us through the Holy Spirit are absolutely incredible: the Lord said to us, under the roof of that tent, presidents and prime ministers will find salvation in Africa. He said, whole nations will become born again – *whole nations*.' Reinhard says, 'I stick to it like glue, even if my mind says it hasn't happened before – I tell you it will happen and we will rejoice because "the earth shall be filled with the knowledge of the glory of the Lord as the waters cover the sea" – whole nations!'

'The Lord said, "You are going to slam right through the iron gates of Islam." I believe it,' says Reinhard. 'We have had a foretaste in Cape Town with over 1,000 Muslims saved when the tent roof blew to bits. The Muslims came and said, "We have cursed your tent–see what has happened!" It was like a public crucifixion to see the tent disintegrate when God had given all these precious promises. It was like a public crucifixion because it happened in front of the eyes of the whole world. The worldly newspapers came and took photos, then on Sunday we saw pictures of our ripped-up tent in colour, blazoned across the newspapers. The news went across the whole country but five days later a new storm burst upon Cape Town, the biggest ever recorded. As the storm hit the city it took the roof off the mosque. It isn't wise to curse those whom God has blessed!'

The tent was fully insured and eventually the CfaN organisation should be reimbursed. It has been proven that the disintegration of the tent was caused by a fabric failure, in the meantime God has provided £600,000 for a replacement tent roof. The promises of God shall be fulfilled as Reinhard sticks to them like glue; through faith and patience he will inherit the promises.

A Mustard Seed of Faith

Are these amazing things happening in South Africa just because God is using outstanding evangelists, or are there other factors?

Without faith it is impossible to please God. The child-like faith of men like Reinhard Bonnke is acting as a strong magnetic pull, drawing the blessings of God upon the nations of Africa. Reinhard says, 'There's no miracle without the word. Faith has to be spoken out.' On one occasion Jesus said to him, 'My word in your mouth, Reinhard, is just as powerful as my word in my mouth.' Like a child he speaks out the word of God and expects sicknesses to go and demons to flee, as if Jesus himself were speaking. Faith doesn't need to be the same size as the problem; Reinhard says, 'A mustard-seed sized faith is enough to blast a mountain. If you've got faith the size of a grain of mustard seed, speak it and use it – it will work.' Reinhard said, 'Faith always needs a catastrophe. It is then that we draw from the deep wells of our spiritual resources and speak words of faith. When catastrophe hits we seek God and hear him. We say what he says, act upon his instructions in obedience and so see the fruits of faith.'

This simple childlike faith has opened the door for God's blessings in South Africa. A growing company of people actually believe that what God says in his word shall be fulfilled; expectation is reaching a new peak – 'God will pour out his Spirit upon all flesh.' Reinhard looks for the word to happen and expects a level of activity in God's harvest field today, such as never before experienced.

In Reinhard's opinion there is a genuine move of the Holy Spirit in South Africa. A divine intervention spreading across denominational barriers, surely a sign of something supernatural. God has his own strategy and at this present time the main emphasis appears to be upon a mighty demonstration of his power. Men like Reinhard Bonnke shrink from exaggerating what God is doing, he says, 'We don't want to magnify peanuts to make them look like potatoes! As the power of God's Spirit is poured out in greater and greater measure we shall move mountains; with the power of God's word in our mouth we shall gain devastating victories over the forces of darkness. The need is weighed in megatons, why must we weigh the answer in ounces? No! We look for the flood-tide of the Spirit of God to sweep across the land. "It's not by might, nor by power, but it's by the Holy Spirit."' Reinhard says, 'I love the Holy Spirit. The task before us will not be accomplished by our ability, but by our availability to the flow and the power of the Holy Spirit within us.'

4: The True Afrikaner

The route into Johannesburg was becoming familiar. We skirted the northern suburbs where the uninteresting dry scrub land looked vulnerable to the relentless urbanisation. The car headed towards Roodepoort where I was to meet Nicky van der Westhuizen. My introduction to his ministry had been when I saw a video recording of him preaching in Durban. I had never seen anything like it before. Squashed up, sitting on the floor in our lounge we were astonished as we watched Nicky, speaking in English, proclaiming God's word in a most audacious way. 'You are for signs and wonders!' he said, taking his Scripture from Isaiah 8:18. Riveted to the screen we heard him say, 'It's no more difficult to speak in tongues than to do a miracle. It's the self same Spirit who causes us to speak in tongues, who also works miracles.' He held everyone's attention in a magnetic grip. This flamboyant, tall young man, striding up and down the long platform passing the microphone from one hand to the other, his open jacket flying as he flung his arm forcefully to make his point, said again, 'You are for signs and wonders!' Our faith was rising, surely he spoke the truth – then to everyone's surprise he demonstrated what he had said.

Calling a young man forward, he showed the congregation how they could release the power of God that is within them, upon another person. As he said, 'I release the power of God,' the Holy Spirit fell upon the young man who crumpled to the floor. After a few moments he got to his feet, looking very drunk. He held on to Nicky whilst he regained his balance. Continuing to explain how to release the power of God into a person's life, Nicky again said, 'And I release the power God has put in me upon the people.' As he spoke, the man still holding on to Nicky, again fell to the ground. His legs appeared to be cut from beneath him as the Spirit of God swamped him. With the lesson demonstrated, faith soared in the congregation at Durban and then they went into action. Watching, we saw the power of the Spirit released among them as they prayed for one another. Miracles happened, dozens came to the microphone to give testimony of healings. These were ordinary members of the congregation who had prayed for one another – released the power of God and seen immediate response. Rising up in faith we saw no reason why we shouldn't do the same at home in our lounge. Tentatively at first, we stepped out and started to pray for one another. We were so excited; God worked among us as we released the Holy Spirit and believed.

With these vivid impressions in my mind, I was thrilled at the prospect of meeting Nicky van der Westhuizen. I stood waiting a little nervously, for Nicky to greet me. Nicky and his wife Rina had kindly invited me to stay for a few days in their home. I was impressed by the quiet peacefulness of the room, enhanced by soft, gentle, colours. The pictures added their own touch of beauty, only to vie with the flowers, arranged so perfectly and as fresh as if they'd just been picked. Nicky then came towards me looking as if he had walked off the video, his fair hair shining and carefully arranged. His appearance was no surprise, tall and slim, with incredibly long legs, wearing a modern looking pale blue suit with matching shoes. Rina followed, looking immaculate but modest, she seemed shy and retiring and rather reluctant to speak English. Their eldest son, about eleven years old, also named Nicky, sat on the settee. He said nothing, perhaps not ready to launch out in English. Nicky seemed an intense, earnest person, passionately devoted to his Lord; one of those people who has a presence about him.

This was my first encounter with the Afrikaners, for them English is a second language but more than that, they have a distinctive culture of their own. In South Africa there are two definite communities among the whites, the Afrikaners and the English. Each have their own traditions, language, food, and a history that reaches back to periods of hostility with each other. The constitution of South Africa has declared Afrikaans and English both official languages to help establish unity. All school children learn both languages but by speaking their mother tongue in their own families the Afrikaner way of life is perpetuated. A large percentage of the white people who live in South Africa's rural areas are Afrikaners. Their small communities centre round the Dutch Reformed Church, with its traditional attitudes and slightly old fashioned way of life. There among the Afrikaners, moral values forgotten by many are clung to in a pharasaical fashion, alongside entrenched apartheid ideas. But even there the buffeting winds of change now threaten the accepted order of past centuries.

Building the Church

As Nicky began to speak, his gentle quiet voice took me by surprise. The lion of a man that I'd seen on the video now seemed like a lamb. He said, 'My principal anointing is as an evangelist. I grew up in a pentecostal denomination and pastored a church until 1979, when God led me into this independent work.' He went on, 'Although I am an evangelist God has told me to build the local church. You cannot imagine the conflict this created in me, because I wanted to be holding campaigns around the country, but constantly I felt this tug back to home base. Praise God that conflict is now past; he's given me rest in his will. I'm happy to be here and build the church.'

The church Nicky is establishing at present meets in a tent at Roodepoort on the Western Rand, a satellite town to Johannesburg. About 2,500 attend the meetings of which

1,000 or so would be committed members. I was interested to know how it had all begun.

Nicky continued, 'It was 1979, when seeking God for the next step in my ministry, the Lord led me to go to Israel to undertake a forty day fast.' During those days God spoke to Nicky with an audible voice and said he purposed to use him for revival in the nation of South Africa. He then instructed him to teach the church on five specific subjects. The Holy Spirit put it in this manner:

- the place of intercession and fasting
- the place of healing and miracles
- the place of praise and worship
- the place of baptism in the Holy Spirit with the anointing of power
- the place of holiness and sanctification in revival

(I sensed as we were talking we stood on holy ground. I was very conscious of the Holy Spirit resting on Nicky, the sweetness of Jesus influenced his whole person. It seemed to accompany him wherever he went and pervaded the very atmosphere of their home, bringing a gentleness and peace so that even I found myself speaking with a softer tone.)

Nicky continued, 'When I began to teach these things, there were about 170 people gathering. The teaching continued over a period of nine to ten weeks. As people came into the anointing the place started to erupt. The hall became so full, more and more people crowded in week by week. It seemed as if revival was breaking out; the church was totally revolutionised!'

With nowhere large enough in which to meet, their only solution was to erect a tent. About 400 people attended the first meetings but within weeks the tent was full. Now the evangelist Nicky found himself confronted with a fantastic problem. He had a new church on his hands; these were his own children, born in his house; he couldn't run off and leave them – yet the evangelist in him wanted to preach the gospel in other towns. The Lord began to give Nicky wisdom to organise his time so that he was not away from the church on a Sunday. From Thursday night to Saturday he may well take evangelistic crusades elsewhere, but on Sundays he comes home to his own church. Sunday morning is a teaching time for the believers; then in the evening the gospel is proclaimed and attested by signs and wonders. The sick come and are healed, the bound are delivered, the unconverted see God at work and are saved.

The congregations are swelled by many who can not be considered part of the church. Desperate people come seeking healing – the curious and enquirers to observe, but God charged Nicky to build the church. What a challenge it has presented. Plans were made to establish house groups, to care for the converts and build them into a strong church. To do this he called upon the aid of Ed Roebert from the Hatfield Baptist Church. He, as a successful pastor, helped by providing house group leadership training. On Sunday mornings Nicky concentrated on teaching commitment and other subjects to strengthen and build the work.

By regularly being in the church and introducing house groups, the local church has become a strong, secure base from which Nicky can discharge his nation-wide ministry. God has given him people who love him, share his evangelistic zeal and passion for revival. The local church, besides providing willing workers, presents a constant challenge to Nicky. They are a group of people for whom he personally takes responsibility. With his finger on the pulse of the church, he senses their need, which drives him to continuously seek the Spirit for fresh revelation. Sunday by Sunday he must bring the word of God to the believers. Nicky said, 'This demand has prevented me from going stale; above everything else, it's driven me to my knees, and kept me spiritually in touch. The travelling evangelist can become very jaded regurgitating eight effective messages from crusade to crusade. The daily claim of the church upon me has been God's tool for my education.'

National Evangelism

As an evangelist, Nicky has a great empathy with the work of Reinhard Bonnke and follows his crusades closely. Nicky shares the conviction of many in South Africa, that the unusual concern and desire for salvation is nothing other than supernatural. Those involved in mass evangelism are experiencing an unprecedented response to the gospel. The crusades are producing fruit, but Nicky asked, 'Is it being built into the churches?' Spiritually hungry people respond to the gospel in an atmosphere where God is at work, but when the crusade team have moved on, so often the local church is spiritually incapable of nurturing, or even attracting the new believers. Despite the lack of spirituality in so many local churches, Nicky has felt that it is not his calling to plant churches where he has crusades, but rather to work with the local churches in such a manner that he makes them spiritually capable of receiving the converts.

When Nicky plans a crusade for a town, it involves a three month investment of his time. First of all, he sends teachers to gather the pastors and at least 500 or so of their people, to be trained in counselling. The teaching goes beyond the ABC of leading someone to the Lord; it is an in-depth affair covering intercession, fasting, faith, the baptism in the Holy Spirit, as well as the normal subjects for counselling in a crusade. His objective is to raise the level of faith among the people and their pastors so that the churches come into a 'new gear', a new level of spiritual experience.

When the last person has left the campaign tent and Nicky has moved on, it is not the end. For the following two months, all who wish to attend – pastors, leaders, counsellors and new converts, are invited to become students at a two-month School of Evangelism. This period of time keeps the group together, establishes them in faith and evangelistic zeal. The eight-week course runs for three nights each week, so it requires commitment. Videos are mixed with live teaching, the aim – to produce students whose lives declare, 'Jesus is alive'. The subjects include intercession and fasting, healing and miracles, praise and worship, the baptism in the Holy Spirit and the anointing of power – the list first given to Nicky by the Lord at the beginning of his ministry. The results are glorious – people are baptised in the Spirit with power and released into fruitful ministry. In 1983, 1,000 students in eight separate groups and working from various locations completed the School of Evangelism. For many it has become the launching pad into a powerful ministry, firing local churches and helping to raise the spiritual temperature in the church of South Africa.

The majority of Nicky's ministry as an evangelist is in the Afrikaans language. When he has a campaign of course it is open for everybody to come, blacks and coloureds alike, but the response is always greater from the whites and his own language group. He has become a highly respected evangelist among many leading Afrikaner church leaders. He has good relationships with denominational churches as well as the new independent fellowships and occasionally gathers groups of pastors together for encouragement. By leaving the pentecostal denomination Nicky sees that God released him to the whole body of Christ. Rather than it being a divisive move, he sees the change clearly as one which makes for unity.

Revival and Prayer

Revival is never far from Nicky's thinking. Our talking ranged widely over many subjects yet the expectancy that God was about to do something vast and breathtaking was never out of focus. Nicky, in common with all his pastors, said, 'Yes we are living in days of revival but there's more to come.' Nicky said, 'God is doing something remarkable in South Africa at the present time.' He had no hesitation in saying, 'This is revival, perhaps not similar to the kind we've experienced in the past but God is being gracious to us and changing our deadness into life.' Like so many other people he emphatically expressed, 'We are living in the last of the last days and preparing for the great, final outpouring of the Holy Spirit.' What we now see in South Africa is part of that preparation. Nicky said, 'These are days of fantastic importance. To enjoy the full benefit of what God is doing, and purposes to do in greater and greater measure, we must co-operate with the Spirit.' (I heard this injunction again and again during my time in South Africa.) The five initial instructions the Holy Spirit gave to Nicky when he embarked upon his new ministry in 1979 are never forgotten. He didn't just teach those things once to the first group and leave it there, no with a holy zeal he continues to teach and exhort in the same vein.

His obedience to the Spirit's instruction to teach the church about prayer, intercession and fasting have led him to make a special place for the ministry of prayer within his own church and organise prayer and intercession on a national basis. Eric Visser as elder at Roodepoort has this responsibility. He has been with Nicky from the very beginning and is like his right hand; a prophet, with a very powerful and perceptive ministry. He travels widely to prepare the ground by prayer in the places where Nicky will hold crusades. As Eric talked, I was impressed by his loyalty and devotion to Nicky.

The following day I had the opportunity of sampling first hand, the church's ministry in prayer. I arrived at the office early with Nicky and was taken in to a small prayer meeting where the staff and ministry team were gathered. They meet every morning for an hour or so. A special room has been set apart for this ministry. It is sound-proofed, a necessary precaution to prevent their neighbours being disturbed! The items for intercession are written up on a blackboard at one end of the room. Pastor Eric Visser provides this direction to those gathered for prayer, who then individually bring these needs to the Lord. As I went into the room, each person was praying individually calling upon God, some with a loud voice, others quietly on their knees, a few standing or sitting, others walking up and down, but each one locked into prayer communion with God. After a while Nicky called the pray-ers to sit down, shared a few words with them, then they went to their daily tasks in the offices, bookshop or printing room. As I talked further with Eric I realised that he was the right person for a nation-wide prayer ministry. He is a man of prayer himself, nothing satisfies him more than being able to shut the door and seek the Lord alone.

The church keeps Friday as a day for fasting and prayer. Unrestricted by timetable, they follow just how the Spirit leads. On Friday nights, they frequently pray through till about two a.m. Throughout the week there are five a.m. prayer meetings and the sisters meet for intercession on Friday mornings. Eric said, 'I find the sisters don't need too much encouragement, they seem more capable of travailing in prayer than the men.' He talked a lot about *travailing*: I listened hard. It's a perspective of prayer I had rarely heard mentioned, is it something we have lost? He described other types of prayer and the way in which he plans for prayer meetings. He said, 'When people are fresh I begin with warfare. Then they have the energy of spirit to rise up against the powers of darkness, and with high praises and worship come right into the presence of God.'

I gathered with the women for prayer. Prayer items were announced and after a short time of praising God, in a most workman-like fashion, immediately they turned to prayer. It was as if they took the burden of the prayer upon themselves, allowing its full weight to rest heavily upon their spirits. They felt the pain and anguish of the situation, and so identified with the need that it became their own. Then out of personal desperation for the situation they cried out to God as women in travail. Their capacity to pray in this fashion amazed me. Among these precious ones God has found some who know how to 'stand in the gap', who know how to come before him on behalf of individuals and even national situations. They were crying out for the Spirit of God to be poured down upon South Africa; for souls to be saved, for solutions to the vast national economic and political problems, for key individuals in government to experience the regenerating power of the Spirit in their lives. These women are bringing a new South Africa to birth in pain, travailing, and anguish: but the pregnant must eventually give birth. Their prayers are fulfilling the Scriptures. They have humbled themselves and sought God's face, surely he will hear from heaven and heal their land. I learned something new that morning, another perspective of the Spirit of God, who can, besides releasing us into joy unspeakable and full of glory, lay his precious ones low in weeping and mourning.

As we left the meeting Eric explained he had developed ways of breaking up prolonged times of prayer into sizeable bites so that the people didn't flag. He said, 'Most people are far more willing to praise and worship than to intercede, therefore I have to encourage the intercession and keep it flowing.' The prayer life of the church is carefully thought out and well organised.

Fasting is taught alongside praying. They have formed chains of prayer and fasting, so at any time there is always someone involved. All their activities are bathed in prayer. Before the services they gather for half an hour and Nicky never goes into an area or church unless the intercessors have first been called together and taught how to pray. For them prayer is a major ministry, they believe in the power of prayer and do not only pay it lip service as some Christians do.

Prayer on the Telephone

Eric introduced me to the round the clock telephone prayer ministry where about 4,000 prayer requests are handled each month. He told me of many notable answers. A woman phoned from hospital where she was dying from cancer: without anyone visiting or laying hands upon her, she was remarkably healed. Others, whilst being prayed for over the telephone have been slain in the Spirit, delivered from demons, and received all manner of answers to prayer. Besides this direct ministry of compassion, part of Nicky's vision is to mobilise prayer across the nation for revival. A faithful army of intercessors are provided with information on a special phone number. At any time they can phone in and get a recorded message of immediate prayer needs. Regular prayer letters, advertising the answers to prayer, encourage the pray-ers. Eric, speaking from his heart said, 'The revival we have will grow, and the revival we long for will come, as we co-operate with the Spirit in deep intercession with travailing and repentance. Soul winning and signs and wonders will increase as we obey the Spirit.'

The emphasis on intercession is absolutely fundamental in everything Nicky does. He said, 'Nothing will happen without intercession. South Africa will not experience a mighty revival unless we pray. We *must* gather the intercessors.' The national network of prayer-warriors are making a major impact upon the country (and those organised from Roodepoort are only one such network).

Recently South Africa, in common with the rest of the continent, has been experiencing drought. During the winter time of 1983, which is the dry season in Johannesburg, a national day of prayer and fasting was called specifically to ask God to send rain. One hundred thousand pamphlets were posted to every corner of the nation. They were put into the hands of the Prime Minister, sent to people of national standing throughout the whole country, secular and otherwise, to every member of the parliament, calling for a national day of prayer and fasting. There was an immediate and positive response.

Five specific issues were taken to the Lord in prayer:

- that it would rain
- that the reservoirs would fill
- that the divorce rate would drop
- that there would be peace on the borders
- that God would send revival

On the chosen day, while they were praying, the heavens opened and it began to rain in Johannesburg, during the dry season! It was national news, God had heard and answered. The reservoirs filled, although the drought continues in many areas of South Africa. The divorce rate has increased with a persistent trend year by year, but the 1983 figure shows an 8% drop – the first time in fifteen years. Praise God! Shortly after the day of prayer, the Mozambique Accord was signed and on the Angolan front there are talks for peace. The God who answered those prayers is also answering their cry for revival.

A Vision

I retreated to my room to assimilate the mass of impressions that had excited and challenged me throughout the day. I started to praise God for what he is doing in South Africa – for gathering intercessors across the nation and the clear answers to prayer that have encouraged them to press on until they see full revival power.

As I waited, the Lord began to show me a vision. In my mind's eye, I seemed to be looking down on a massive aerial view of South Africa. Nicky, like a giant, stood with his feet astride the Rand. Stretching southwards from where he stood, through the heartland of South Africa and down towards Cape Town; I saw a huge, long, white tablecloth. Scattered across the tablecloth were many little delicate moulds made of a white substance similar to flour. They looked like individual jellies, or sand-pies that children make on the beach. On closer examination I knew each represented a church. Nicky picked up his end of the tablecloth, and shook it. Every fragile mould disintegrated leaving little mounds of white dust all the way down to Cape Town. The Lord said to me, 'I'm shaking everything that can be shaken.'

It would be comforting if God sat in heaven and did the shaking, but in fact he uses men. As the ministry of faith flows from his life and from others similarly baptised with the Holy Spirit *and power*, it is causing repercussions in the church. I suppose we shouldn't be surprised, throughout history, whenever the Holy Spirit has come in power, he has caused a shaking. The dead formalism of many traditional churches is being jolted by manifestations of God's power, which in turn have created a new hunger among church members. Now they're being baptised in the Holy Spirit, and that means they are no longer satisfied with a church whose life is words, but no power; form, but no life. Loyalty to the old ways is being shaken as many people discover a new loyalty to Jesus himself. They are leaving the old churches and migrating to the large new ones or joining one of the hundreds of smaller fellowships that are springing up in most communities. Elijah couldn't have found it easy to be 'a troubler' in Israel, and even though Ahab feared him, he knew who had the answers.

Proclamation and Demonstration

Eagerly I looked forward to the opportunity of attending a Sunday meeting at The Big Tent. We drove right out of town and passed the slag-heaps, man made creamy mountains of discarded ore and rubble from the gold mines. Somehow they looked tidier than the slag-heaps about coal pit-heads. The car swung round a bend and there in front of us, was a large striped tent on some waste land, far away from any habitations. To me it seemed an odd place to have a meeting, but obviously the hundreds of people drawing up in their cars didn't think so. South Africans are prepared to travel quite a few miles for meetings. It was a cold evening as we went inside, but the tent was already warmed by the crowd of bodies seated waiting for the meeting to begin. Looking about me it seemed as if the clock had been turned back to about the nineteen-sixties. The Afrikaners are quite old fashioned in their dress. The women wear lacy veils, fussy hats, gloves and clothes which portray a modesty of a past era. Most men wore respectable 'Sunday' suits and even young children were dressed for the occasion. I've never seen such well turned out little boys.

During the winter months the second Sunday meeting is held in the afternoon rather than the evening, otherwise the congregation's cold feet might numb their responsiveness. These occasions are for evangelism and praying for the sick. Nicky believes that his work has grown so phenomenally because of the signs and wonders ministry. He said, 'The people come for the miracles.' It was the same in the days of Jesus; he demonstrated that he had the answer to life's problems. People haven't changed, nor have their needs. Miracles still draw a crowd.

The musicians took their seats. Wearing a sort of uniform, they looked rather like happy undertakers with smart dark suits, red hankies in their pockets, and identical ties; perhaps more suited to a symphony orchestra than a gospel band! Not a glum face was to be seen, all were wreathed in smiles, rejoicing.

The music began – the tent erupted into joyful singing and noisy praise. The rather stiff looking congregation were immediately liberated – singing at the tops of their voices, shouting, praising, clapping their hands, dancing and jumping about. Dressed as they were it looked incongruous, but proved uninhibited praise is not limited to a certain kind of person! The spirit of praise and worship was beautiful and exuberant.

Casting out Devils

The Afrikaners have a long history of pentecostalism and probably a good number of Nicky's congregation that

Sunday afternoon originally came from those churches. The tent was absolutely full, looking about me, I could see they were obviously in need of a 5,000-seater tent or a permanent building. Nicky wearing a pale coloured suit and a pink shirt looked most relaxed and beamed at the people as he led the singing. Taking Mark 1:39 as his text, he began to carefully teach about demon possession. Sitting back, I prepared to soak in every syllable; I didn't want to miss anything.

He said, 'Jesus came to cast out devils! When you see devils being cast out, it is evidence that the kingdom of God has come. Then the dominion of darkness is seen to be overcome by the power of God.' Step-by-step he clearly described what demon possession really means. 'We all imagine a possessed person must be like a raving lunatic,' he said, 'but the word that is translated *possession* in our Bibles can mean "being under the control of", or "being attacked", or just "being harassed".' Nicky said, 'Many Christians think they're not prone to this kind of interference but I tell you, the devil is no respecter of persons and he goes around like a roaring lion seeking someone to devour. You can only be free from his interference and harassment if you walk right.'

Nicky continued, 'Anyone who openly confronts the devil is not going to be short of critics, they will appear even from among the ranks of Christians, but Jesus sent his disciples to cast out demons.' How can the kingdom of God be established if we fail to obey this injunction? He continued, 'Let me encourage you; you have authority within yourselves to overcome the harassment of demons.' Using the illustration of Legion, who ran to Jesus and worshipped him, Nicky said, 'Our wills are stronger than demons, even the man with legion had the power to choose to worship Jesus.' He explained, we too can decide by setting our wills to get free from the onslaught of the evil one in our lives and serve God.

The teaching about demon possession prepared the way

to cast out demons. Through a word of knowledge, Nicky first called people forward who had a desire to commit suicide. Two walked on to the platform but he was sure there were two others, they responded and he limited it to just those four people. Two were drug addicts. He prayed for each of them, commanding the spirits to leave, there were no tremendous demonic manifestations, two fell down under the power of the Holy Spirit, and two stayed standing. It took only a few moments and certainly wouldn't have satisfied those who were looking for something spectacular.

Turning from the four, he addressed the congregation and invited those who wished to be free from uncontrollable emotions, such as anger and jealousy, to stand at the front. Dozens and dozens of people walked forward. Each was joined by a counsellor, who at Nicky's instruction laid his hands upon the person as Nicky spoke a word of deliverance. Almost as soon as he opened his mouth to pray, demons were being manifested. It looked like total confusion at the front of the church, with people falling down, shouting, screaming and being thrown around as demons were evicted by the word of authority. I wouldn't have thought one of those people expected to behave in that manner, but as someone has said, 'You either keep your dignity or your demons!' Demons slip in quietly, but they do like to make a fuss when they leave! The unholy confusion was soon quietened – the people returned to their places as a few gave testimony – God had set them free. What an amazing sight! About seventy people delivered from demons at once. Authority over demons would relieve pastors of so many problems and save them a lot of time!

Praying for the Sick

Then came the time for praying for the sick. When I had looked for a vacant seat at the beginning of the meeting I noticed a mother cradling a sleeping child in her arms – he had deaf aids in both ears. During the service the child wakened and she carried him outside. I hurriedly looked around to find her because brother Nicky was calling the deaf to come forward – he would pray for them. Unfortunately the woman was nowhere to be seen, but a young boy of about twelve or thirteen, right from the back of the tent walked up on to the stage. From birth he had suffered with ear trouble and despite many operations had become totally deaf. Nicky, placing his fingers in the boy's ears, commanded the deaf spirit to leave. He removed his fingers and a look of amazement went across the boy's face. He could hear. Brother Nicky wished to be thoroughly satisfied about his healing, so he tested him carefully with whispers and very slight noises. The boy heard everything! Then he called his father to also test him. The man was incredulous – God had done a miracle. The congregation clapped their hands and loudly praised God.

Faith rose. Then in that atmosphere of faith Nicky called the cancer sufferers to come forward. Three desperately sick people were helped to the front. An elderly man sitting in a wheelchair said he had lung cancer yet still smoked three cigarettes a day. We joined hands and all prayed at once as Nicky and three others laid their hands upon him. The man got up out of his wheelchair and started to walk. With each step he seemed stronger. He walked and walked up and down in front of the meeting. The whole congregation rose to their feet craning their necks, shouting praises and encouragement. The old man's back straightened, he gained confidence, he was being healed. While continuing to walk, he began to look very intently at his left hand, which was covered by a sock. I could almost see him thinking. Without stopping he carefully pulled the sock off to show a badly deformed hand and arm held in a spastic position. Staring hard at his paralysed hand, he was willing it to move, then his stiff, wax-like fingers flickered. Then he attempted to open the hand fully and raise his arm. The locked joints began to move, he persevered and little by little the paralysed deformed arm became free. Glory to God, the people were shouting and praising the Lord. Then he swung it far above his head, and looked on incredulously as his once solid, fixed arm moved and did what he wanted it to do; all the time he never stopped walking! He pushed his wheelchair away and sat on an ordinary chair.

Nicky exhorted him, 'Keep on acting out your faith, keep on doing what you couldn't do before!' The people were on their feet arms raised, tears streaming down many faces praising God for the glorious miracle they had just seen. It was in this atmosphere that Nicky called those to respond who wished to receive Jesus as Lord and Saviour. The unsaved had seen that Jesus is alive and without hesitation declared their faith.

Points to Ponder

- *What makes it God's time for South Africa?*
- *Can we by prayer make it 'God's time for our nation?' 'If my people who are called by my name humble themselves, and pray and seek my face, and turn from their wicked ways; then I will hear from heaven, and forgive their sin and heal their land.' 2 Chron. 8:14.*
- *Why do hundreds of thousands of Christians baptised in the Holy Spirit lack the dimension of power seen in the Acts of the Apostles? The Bible says, 'You shall receive* ***power*** *after the Holy Spirit has come upon you.' Acts 1:8.*

5: Mr Universe has a Big Heart

I'd heard a lot about the 'Rhema' people. The car drew up at the back of some shops and the driver directed me to the entrance. 'Welcome to Rhema Bible Church' said the receptionist. 'I've an appointment to see Ray McCauley.' She beckoned me to the sofa and I waited – wondering what kind of person I was going to meet. Ray, with his wife Lynda, had founded the Rhema Bible Church (South Africa) in 1979; besides a local church it is a leading organisation with increasing influence in the nation. The 'Rhema Churches' which originate in the United States of America are proliferating all over the world. As their name implies, the word of God is central in their teaching – 'Rhema' meaning a specific word.

Being a Bible-believing Christian myself I thought, 'Isn't the word of God central in our churches also?' What's the difference? Their emphasis appeared to imply 'something more than average Bible believing' – whatever that may be.

Most denominations and Christian movements are birthed in particular revelations. The special new insight into God's word is very precious to the discoverer and later to those who benefit from it. Being inquisitive and always ready to sample more of God in whatever wrapping he hides himself, I put out my spiritual antennae. 'Lord please show me the particular truth the Holy Spirit is presenting through the Rhema Churches.' Life is too short for us to personally discover everything for ourselves, so others' 'choice finds' are always an attraction for me. I was in

South Africa with an open mind ready to give glory to God wherever I saw him working.

Ray came round his desk to greet me as I entered his office. Immediately I liked him – a thick built, warm-hearted looking man with a shiny face; I guessed in his mid-thirties. He beamed, shook hands and made me feel completely at ease.

Chatting naturally he began to tell me a little of himself. Before his conversion in 1977 he had been a 'body builder' – not of vehicles but of physique and muscle! His success in South Africa brought the 'Mr Universe' title within reach. All the energy and discipline of that past life is now switched to a vigorous pursuit of God's will for his life, where he needs all his strength to keep pace with God's rigorous programme. Since his conversion there has been no stopping. Like a rocket going into orbit, Ray has taken off with his life faithfully tracing a pre-ordained path.

Rhema Bible Church

In 1978 with his wife Lynda, Ray attended the Rhema Bible training centre in Tulsa, Oklahoma, USA, where God gave him the vision for reaching Africa for Jesus. After completing their training, they returned to South Africa and in Ray's parents' home led their first meeting with about fifteen people present. From that small beginning has mushroomed an ever expanding work with thousands converted, a church of thousands in Randburg and hundreds of other churches in South Africa relating to Rhema Ministries. It is impossible to guess the number also healed and delivered.

The work seemed to get off the ground with a big bang. In just eighteen months there were three services each Sunday to cater for 2,500 people in the much overcrowded 700-seater cinema rented for their meetings. A move to a bigger theatre in the centre of Johannesburg was God's provision till March 1981 when they took possession of a renovated three storey shopping block, with the ground floor beautifully reconstructed to provide offices, bookshop, tape and video centres, wholesale book depot, Bible schools, counselling facilities and a large auditorium (that's a story in itself).

When God is at work nothing is static – in no time at all it was obvious another move would have to be made. On 1st November 1982 thirty-two acres of land were purchased to make a permanent base for Rhema Ministries, South Africa. Now a new building is being constructed with a 5,000-seater auditorium, two separate halls for 500 and 900 people, plus all the other facilities required for an organisation and church touching the whole of South Africa – with its eyes on the rest of the continent for Jesus. The new building will be officially opened in June 1986. The vision is big and big steps of faith are taken to make it reality.

Dr Kenneth E. Hagin who will be participating in the opening ceremony has been present at each major step forward in the work. I was touched by the loving way in which Ray spoke of Kenneth Hagin, he said he owed him an impossible debt of gratitude. Among men, Kenneth Hagin, more than any other has provided the inspiration, teaching, vision, anointing and faith to prosper the work.

We were talking of spiritual things in the most ordinary fashion. I looked at Ray's hands – strong and muscular – doer's hands, I could imagine him grabbing a heavy log with the greatest of ease and sawing it for the fire. Jesus' hands were familiar with wood, a common-place commodity, he knew where to make the best cut, how to enhance the grain of the wood, he understood its properties. Ray in the same masterly fashion has a 'feel' for the spiritual realm. As he touches and handles things unseen he does it as a devoted craftsman, one with experience.

I asked Ray, 'To what do you attribute the amazing growth here at Rhema?' A thoughtful look flashed across his face, then he said in a decided tone, 'It's the demonstration of power. You see, when I returned after a year in Bible School, an anointing came upon my ministry. How can I describe it in any other way? It's the Holy Spirit, he began to move through me powerfully confirming the word with signs and wonders. Yes of course I had been baptised in the Holy Spirit but this was a new dimension. If you come to our meetings you will see what I mean. There is something to be seen. Theological concepts and Bible knowledge are shaken into life by the demonstration of God's power.' I thought for a moment; crowds followed Jesus because they *saw* the works he did; this sounded the same.

In the first year of their ministry in Randburg, 27,000 people were saved! It goes without saying, Ray's an evangelist. Out of those first time decision cards sixty per cent were not from local people. News spread, something was happening over at Randburg and crowds came to have a look, were saved and then went back, possibly to their home churches or to form the nucleus of one of the many new churches springing up.

Although in those early days, thousands of people were saved, healed and delivered through the ministry, a powerful voice began to speak violently against the work. Some went so far as to say, 'It is of the devil!' As an independent church, it didn't fit into the normal pattern of things. South Africa has a long tradition of good Pentecostal churches and a variety of others which have become like part of the landscape, so many asked, 'Why form a new denomination?' Pentecostal groups began to feel insecure when some of their most promising people joined the new work.

As I walked around the flourishing complex of offices, visited the Dean of the Bible School and the School of Psalmody, at every turn the logo of the Rhema Bible Churches confronted me. A little shield with the word 'faith' superimposed. Every aspect of the work I visited was the fruit of faith. Browsing in the bookshop, its bountifully stocked shelves were laden with books on faith, books I had never seen before including some old ones whose teaching and inspiration made them worth their weight in gold. Faith was taught as well as talked, was evident in works as well as words.

South Africa is a religious nation, God is honoured and believed in by the majority. Church attendance is high but large numbers of church-goers are not born again. The Charismatic movement has been powerful in South Africa particularly among the Anglicans. Its impact rocked many stable traditional churches. Now, in the wake of its waning, the 'faith ministry' for want of a better name, is growing where it would have been unheard of, only five years ago.

Confessing the Word

The work at Rhema is built upon the Hagin faith principles. The word of God is taught in an intensely practical fashion, and never just for knowledge to puff men's minds – but for doing. The word of God dwells in them richly as they cultivate the habit of reading, meditating, memorising and confessing its truth, to themselves, to God, and the devil. They persist in simple childlike repetition of the truth until the words instruct their spirits and undo natural unbelief. Release then comes and ability to really believe the truth of the word of God. It is like brain-washing unbelieving hearts with the truth of God. The only effect it can have is good, for the Bible says, 'The truth shall set you free.'

Great emphasis is laid upon 'what you say'; 'positive speaking'; 'being trapped by your words'; 'the power of the spoken word'; 'confessing yourself out of a situation'. This teaching springs from Mark 11:23, 'Truly, I say to you whoever says to this mountain, "Be taken up and cast into the sea", and does not doubt in his heart, but believes that what he *says* will come to pass, it will be done for him.'

The teaching stresses, what you *say* will happen, what you confess with your mouth will come to pass, therefore be careful what you say, make positive confession, and live in the blessing of God. Obviously the immature can distort such teaching so as to make Paul look a failure when he was beaten, stoned and run out of town again and again!

A simple example of how this affects praying is to be found in Kenneth Hagin's book, *How You Can Be Led By The Spirit of God*, on page seventy-four, when he was praying for a woman whose faith sagged because she 'felt' nothing, and I quote, 'Dear Lord, I'm so glad that I'm a child of God, I'm so glad that I'm saved, I'm so glad that I've been born again. I don't feel anything but that has nothing to do with it. My inward man is a new man, my inward man is a new creature in Christ. I want to thank you that I'm not only born again but I'm filled with the Holy Spirit. God the Father, God the Son, and God the Holy Spirit reside in me. I want to thank you for that. Hallelujah!' The simplicity of such confession could appear meaningless but its results are profound. Here's another example from Ray McCauley in an article, 'Following in the Footsteps of Jesus' from *Eagle News* dated October/November 1984. 'We have to speak the word only, not what we feel, nor what the circumstances seem, not what we think. We should say but the word only. For example "I dwell in the secret place of the Most High, I dwell under the shadow of the Almighty, I will say of the Lord, he is my fortress and my refuge, in him I trust because he is able to do exceedingly abundantly above all that I ask according to the power which works in me. The Lord is my shepherd, I shall not want for wisdom, I shall not want for understanding. The love of God is shed abroad in my heart, I am longsuffering, I am kind, I thank you Father that you wish above all things that I prosper and be in good health. Thank you Father that my mind is renewed to the word of God. I am not conformed to this world but I'm transformed by the renewing of my mind. I thank you that you've come to give life to me and life more abundantly and that whatever I put my hand to will prosper. I'm speaking your word only today Lord Jesus and I thank you that as I do so it will not return empty but it shall accomplish that which I have sent it out to do. I thank you that you have given me favour with God and man and though I'll walk through the valley of the shadow of death I will fear no evil. Fear is far from me because the love of God is perfected in me and I thank you that I submit myself, humble myself under your mighty hand and resist the devil and he flees."' With such words of truth in our mouths who can fall?

As you can imagine this almost simplistic attitude to the Scriptures and childlike way of confessing their truth has found its opponents. 'Rhema' are accused of having 'gone over the top' on faith and having an unintelligent attitude towards the word of God. Their opponents allege this form of confession brings people into bondage if they fail to receive what they're believing for: and it encourages carnality, as people only pray for possessions and money. Of course all spiritual activities can either be of faith or degenerate into dead works. There is no guarantee that that which even began in faith will automatically remain so, except faith is daily stirred up and received. Possibly many who discovered this means of possessing their possessions in Christ, have used their faith to gain material things rather than spiritual – but to put it into perspective, often financial possessions are more tangibly recognisable as evidence of answered prayer than spiritual advances.

A Prosperity Cult?

Ray was very ready to talk about his attitude to prosperity. He said, 'We have been accused of being a prosperity cult. It's true we've talked prosperity and have become prosperous. What a shame that success in some things does not bring admiration. It's a spiritual breakthrough to possess finance for the work of God.' Ray went on to say, 'My attitude to prosperity is fundamentally a spiritual, scriptural one. I lay great emphasis on prosperity in every aspect of life including health, spiritual abilities, as well as finance. God is not blessed by us being poor. He intends us to be prosperous in every area of our lives. All the abilities that God gives are to further his work and not for our own satisfaction.' When that emphasis is laid deeply in people's hearts we see that prosperity is an important ability to further the kingdom of God. Prosperity which blesses every area of life speaks volumes to our needy world. Ray went on to say, 'Prosperity is essential,' and he said, 'but let me define what I mean by prosperity; *it's the ability to meet any given need at any given time.*' We are involved in God's work. The plans are his and the bills are his. God intends to provide for his work and our eyes are on him alone. If we seek first the kingdom of God he will supply every need.

The Pitfalls of Faith Teaching

Like every good thing when taken too far, faith teaching can produce some unfortunate reactions. When a group really believe 'that I can do all things through Christ who strengthens me', the '*I*' can become very large in some people's minds. '*I can*' encourages independence and attracts strong independent people whilst at the same time, let's not forget, it remains God's incentive to motivate us in ministry.

As Ray began to establish the church at Randburg, the rebellious and independent made their presence felt. He taught submission and the authority of God-given leadership in the church, to bring a balance to those with independent zeal desperate to rush off 'to do their own thing', be their own judge and master.

For Ray, an evangelist, to give this kind of teaching was a new experience, but a 'church building' ministry which lays a firm foundation, was essential. For the first time he taught about family life and the fruit of the Spirit. He is supplementing the original emphasis of faith for signs, wonders, healing, salvation, growth and financial provision with teaching that builds character and true spirituality. To help lay these foundations visiting speakers are also invited.

Those who only come to see amazing signs and to experience something of the power of God in their lives, are not readily captured by a teaching ministry. They stay away on those evenings. Ray is not easily despondent over such things. His eyes are upon the future. With careful building now, the church which is rapidly growing, will hold together and be able to build the new converts into its life. This new dimension to Ray's ministry is a valuable addition to his gifting and understanding. Building the church has become an instruction to him, providing the opportunity to expand his abilities.

Competitiveness is another pitfall opened up by faith teaching. A material blessing, which can be shown off, is one of the quickest ways to prove one's faith. It's quite laughable really, but because we're human these are the kind of traps we fall into.

Victor Mundy, who is the Dean of the Rhema Bible School, put it very beautifully. When in England both he and another brother staying in a house together were without transport. You can imagine – both were praying hard. A few days later someone came to Victor's friend, and said, 'The Lord has directed me to give you a car', and the following day a beautiful Mercedes arrived on the parking place outside! Victor prayed on. Soon his prayers were answered, and a motorcycle was delivered! The kind donor said, 'This is what the Lord has told me to give to you.' There on the same parking place outside their home was the Mercedes and the motorcycle, next to one another. Victor said, 'Look how things have changed. Wow! A few years ago I would have been churned up, feeling a failure. Such a situation would have caused real trouble. I would have smarted as the accusing finger pointed, saying, "Look, your faith must be smaller than his, you've only got a motorbike!"' Victor said, 'That day was evidence to us that we had grown in grace. None of those horrible things happened. We could both give thanks for whatever the Lord had provided.'

The Means of Growth

Let me tell you a little bit more about the church. Like all fast growing churches, whatever one writes, it's out of date by the time it's in print. The most oustanding example is Full Gospel Central Church in Seoul, Korea, where last month's statistics are as dead as last year's Christmas cards. At the Rhema Bible Church in Johannesburg they have about 400 new converts each week. One of the major criticisms of churches like Rhema which are built by evangelists, is that those saved on Sunday are out the 'back door' on Monday! – that they are incapable of holding the catch. Worldly logic assumes that the converts were not genuine in the first place. Men like Ray are only too aware of their need to build the church and pastor the people, so that they stay and grow. To this end Ray involves every department of the church.

When people respond in the meetings they are taken into a side hall where they have a few words of instruction and counsel. A decision card is filled out and passed on to one of the home group leaders within forty-eight hours, who then endeavours to meet with the new convert. Once a person has responded to the gospel in a meeting, the major task of seeing them built into the church is taken on by the home cells. Unlike many churches, the home cells at Rhema Bible Church are principally run to care for the new believers. During each weekly meeting fifteen to twenty minutes is spent on a new believers' course covering fifteen lessons. All the groups do the same lesson material and repeat it again and again. The remaining part of the cell group time is for questions and fellowship. In such a large church, meeting together in small groups is essential for the making and keeping of loving relationships.

With the variety of activities provided by the church there is every opportunity for the new believer to grow. The Bible school has two separate groups, one in the morning and one in the evening. The full time course for ten months is complete in itself but for those desiring further study there is an extra year. The students are in class work for three hours and then the rest of their time is taken with their assignments. The syllabus is Kenneth Hagin's material from the Tulsa Bible School but slightly adapted for South Africa's needs. Apart from these two full time courses there are also 500 students involved in a correspondence school. In the advertising material the Bible School is called a 'Supernatural School, which is led by the supernatural'. It makes no attempt to be a theological institution. The whole emphasis of the teaching is to bring the word of God to the students in such a way that it becomes a living reality by the Spirit. It's a glorious aspiration. Victor Mundy said they desire that the word should be made so alive to the students that they become walking testimonies displaying the power of God. He said, 'An anointing comes upon them as they are taught. God is at work among us.' As the Spirit leads they prophesy and pray for them individually and send them out into ministry, fired and envisioned with the promises of God.

This radical Bible school has its opponents, but the proof of the rightness of their approach can be measured by the high percentage of students who go into successful full time ministry. Forty-eight of the first fifty students are now serving God. Some of the leading men in South Africa came straight out of the Rhema Bible School. Victor Mundy himself was one of the first students. Theo Wolmerans who leads Christian City, perhaps the largest church in Johannesburg, also attended the Rhema Bible School as one of the first students. Provoked by its success, pastors from the Assemblies of God came to see how it was accomplished. Theology lecturers have come and even wept, as they realised they were incapable of teaching anything other than Greek, Hebrew, and theological knowledge; whereas here they discovered students, who in addition to these subjects, also received an anointing of wisdom and power for their ministry. Students come from all over South Africa and from abroad. Victor said that at one time they had seventeen different denominations represented in one class, then added, 'As these students sit and learn together they are being drawn together. I see the school as a unifying influence in the body of Christ.'

I had to smile to myself as Victor said, 'We have many invited teachers and speakers into the Bible school so as to provide a broad spectrum of teaching.' He then mentioned those who have spoken to the students on evangelism; Reinhard Bonnke and Nicky van der Westhuizen and other thoroughly dynamic evangelists whose ministry is accompanied by signs and wonders – hardly a broad spectrum! I'm certain Victor considered they were giving a perfectly balanced view, because the Bible says, Jesus sent his disciples out to preach the gospel, heal the sick, cast out demons, raise the dead – and he said it all in one breath. The preaching of the gospel was never supposed to be divorced from signs, deliverances and healings; in truth there is not another gospel that can be preached.

Done with Excellence

To run a church efficiently with a congregation in the thousands takes a lot of hard work and self-sacrificing effort from many people. The standard of serving at Rhema was exemplary. The stewards were easily recognisable, all immaculately dressed in a uniform maroon blazer. They are there well before the meetings begin arranging the chairs and praying over each one, removing chewing gum from beneath the seats and generally making the place look inviting for everyone who walks in. Their duties are full and varied including catching those who are slain in the Spirit! They are the fount of all knowledge and would match the efficiency of a doorman at the Dorchester Hotel.

Ray had talked to me honestly about every conceivable aspect of the church's life, but nothing can be as instructive as feeling it for oneself. On Wednesday night I decided to attend the first of Ray's teachings on the fruit of the Spirit. People arrived early and spent time browsing in the bookshop and talking in small groups. There seemed to be a lot of friendly chatter. As I watched the people take their seats, there were far more blacks in the congregation than I had seen in any other group. Quite a number were sitting round about me but I wondered if a few of the young fellows had come in because of the cold. They looked extremely poor, dirty, and were very smelly – almost overpoweringly so. Fortunately it appeared to be no hindrance to many loving souls, black and white, who welcomed them and went out of their way to show kindness.

After worshipping the Lord for a time, the offering was announced. It's their habit to take offerings whenever the people come together. Prosperity teaching seems to go hand in hand with a larger willingness to give. Hence, offerings at every meeting and generous, open-hearted congregations. The leader of the meeting read Luke 6:38, 'Give and it will be given to you, good measure, pressed down, shaken together, running over, will be put into your lap for the measure you give will be the measure you get back.' (Passing the collecting boxes was not going to be a hurried affair.) Taking his time he beautifully expounded the Scripture, emphasising the way the Lord gives back to us as we give. To illustrate he said, 'When a blood donor gives blood, he doesn't give it expecting to receive it back, but his body naturally makes up the loss without him having to do anything, or even ask. So it is with the Lord; using the same measure with which we give, he gives back to us.'

In a leisurely manner he then illustrated how God delights to give to us. In 1 Kings 3, Solomon was invited to ask the Lord for whatever he wanted; he requested wisdom.

God, out of his infinite riches, not only gave him wisdom, but abundantly prospered him and showered him with wealth above any other. God's desire to give to us is beyond what we ask and far beyond our needs. Our attention was drawn to eternal values, 'But seek first his kingdom and his righteousness and all these things shall be yours as well', Matthew 6:33. With this verse of Scripture in mind, everyone held their offering in their hand before the Lord, thanked him for the ability to give and his promise to meet every need. The manner in which this offering was taken became an instruction in itself, all done in a beautiful spirit and surprisingly, provided the perfect preparation for the ministry of the word.

Ray taught very simply but effectively on the fruit of the Spirit. At one point, by using different members of the congregation, he acted out how the fruit of the Spirit, when it is developed in a believer's life, becomes his defence against strong temptations and satanic attacks. As soon as he had finished preaching, an invitation was given for anybody who wished to be saved. Thirty to forty people walked to the front. I found it quite surprising as it certainly hadn't been an evangelistic message. (While we were talking Ray had said to me, 'You should always give the opportunity for people to be saved, even if you only do it for practice!') Ray stood on the platform, praising God for these 'precious ones', as he called them. Two or three times he said it, and by the tone of his voice I felt he meant it with all his heart. There were alcoholics, down-and-outs, people whose desperate state could not be hidden, blacks, whites – sad, lonely, lost men and women in need of Jesus. The special love of the evangelist was being showered upon the converts as they walked to the front, not only were they precious in God's sight, but in the eyes of all the people, as they shared Ray's delight in those who responded to the gospel. Ray invited some of the congregation to come and express the love that they all felt for them. Men, women, and whole families hurried forward and mingled with the slightly awkward group standing at the front. It was beautiful to see. Culture and colour meant nothing, everyone was hugging one another, praising God for his salvation.

There seemed a real expectation that people would be converted quite regardless of what is preached. The sheer delight shown by the congregation towards those who respond, has been caught from Ray, whose love for souls influences all the people. Whilst the group were led away to be counselled, the meeting continued. Through the word of knowledge, certain individuals were brought to a response to the teaching just received. Their works of the flesh were exposed; jealousy, hatred and uncontrolled anger. The word of knowledge came with power, bringing obvious repentance. Many were slain in the Spirit instantaneously as they were prayed for.

Being Slain in the Spirit

Travelling through the churches in South Africa, almost without exception, I saw people falling down under the power of the Spirit countless times. Did they fall down because that was expected? A minority may do but the testimony of thousands tells another story. One woman said, 'The power of God came heavily upon me, swamping all natural senses. I fell, although I was hardly aware of falling and I didn't hurt myself. Whilst lying on the floor my spirit seemed so alive and awake. Inside I was laughing and crying all at once with the sheer wonder of God's presence. I felt bathed in love. God was speaking to me, although I can't fully remember what he said. He was speaking in my spirit and my mind didn't take it all in. After a while I became aware of others around me but I didn't want to get up as I felt I would be walking out of the amazing intimacy I was enjoying with God. My skin felt tingling with a pleasant warm burning sensation, but that was peripheral – beyond everything else the awareness of God himself was intense and there was no fear in it.'

At first it appeared to be the most amazing phenomenon: people collapsing as if anaesthetised with only a light touch upon their heads. At a glance one would think they were asleep or even in a coma. Some fall to the ground without any physical contact, others appear to be picked up and thrown by an unseen power. Some may find it frightening whilst others are awe-struck at the sight of normal rational people behaving in the most unpredictable manner. The unspiritual man is naturally baffled by this kind of happening in the lives of sane, ordinary human beings. It is strange, embarrassing and cannot be explained, it seems extravagant and unnecessary to many Christians.

Is it the latest fad – the next 'in thing' now that we have got used to the idea of speaking in tongues? Only a small investigation in the Bible will reveal that falling down in the presence of the power of God is no new thing. It disappeared from normal church life when the powerful presence of God was no longer a reality, but today, as God pours out his Spirit, not only in South Africa but all around the world, again people are falling under the power of the Spirit.

When Jesus was met in the Garden of Gethsemane by Judas and his companions, Jesus asked them in John 18:4, 'Whom do you seek?' They answered him, 'Jesus of Nazareth.' Jesus said to them, 'I am he.' As soon as he said, 'I am he', they went backward and fell to the ground. These men were on an important errand – to take Jesus captive. The last thing they would naturally do, was to fall to the ground. The chief priests and captains fell down against their own will, unable to stand in God's presence. You may expect Jesus to have had that effect upon people, but do you remember how the glory of God came and filled Solomon's Temple at its dedication? What an atmosphere there must have been – praise, worship, instruments and voices raised to magnify the Lord. Then he came. The house was filled with a cloud so that the priests could not stand, for the glory of the Lord had filled the house of God. They couldn't stand up – God had come, not in physical form, but in the power of his presence.

Throughout the history of the church, in unusual visitations of the Spirit, people have fallen down under the power of God. It happened in Wesley's days, during the Finney revivals, and more recently in the Hebrides revival. We read in Duncan Campbell's account of those remarkable days in 1949, 'Here is a scene witnessed during the first days of the movement: a crowded church, the service is over: the congregation, reluctant to disperse, stand outside the church in a silence that is tense. Suddenly a cry is heard within: a young man, burdened for the souls of his fellow-men, is pouring out his soul in intercession. He prays until he falls into a trance and lies prostrate on the floor of the church. But heaven had heard, and the congregation, moved by a power that they could not resist, came back into the church, and a wave of conviction of sin swept over the gathering, moving strong men to cry to God for mercy.' (*God's Answer*. Published by The Faith Mission 1960, now out of print.)

Doesn't the re-emergence of this phenomenon signal that God has come? With a new intensity, he is making his presence known among his people. I pray the days will come when the magnitude of his power will so increase it will cause us all to fall to the floor as in Solomon's day, and cry out like Isaiah when he saw the Lord in the purity of his holiness.

People are healed miraculously as they lie on the floor under the power of God. Others receive new anointings of the Spirit for service, some rise to their feet speaking in tongues, prophesying or seeing visions. A few are totally overwhelmed by the Spirit and enter a trance, like Peter did on the roof top at Simon's house in Acts chapter ten. What can we say except, 'It's God!'

Hitting the Headlines

Rhema Bible Church has hit the news. Ray says, 'This is a controversial church, continuously the media and the newspapers are on the phone. They want to know what we are doing and investigate the claims to healings. Spiritual manifestations are a curiosity – that makes them newsworthy. Yesterday they wanted my opinion about a new import into South Africa, a Waddington's ouija board, a game for children. Of course I didn't give my own opinion, I quoted Deuteronomy to them,' said Ray. 'It's amazing – they keep coming again and again. There's a perpetual enquiry about the "born again" people these days, they want to know how we react to certain events and news items. You can be sure not all the press we get is flattering! Did you know, even employers are asking those coming for jobs, "are you born again?" Some are really keen to have Christians, they're sought-after workers, but others don't want that kind of person around! I guess it depends on their business, they would be a thorn in the flesh in some shady companies.'

Supernatural happenings like healings and miracles are guaranteed to stir up reactions. There is always a group who want to prove it didn't really happen, or the way it took place was wrong, or that it was of the devil! When Ray prays for the sick he has such a childlike simple approach to the Scriptures, it is bound to annoy some. He says, the Bible teaches us God intends to heal everyone. In the same manner as he longs to save everyone – although not everyone is saved – his intention is to heal everyone, although all may not get healed. He preaches fearlessly that salvation and healing are in the cross and cannot be separated. By the death of Jesus we receive life and by his stripes we are healed. Ray calls the sick forward proclaiming God will heal them. He said, 'There'll always be a critic sitting in the congregation who says, "Well how can he say that, when there are people there who are not healed? He's simplistic, not facing the facts."' Unbelief does not change the word of God. Ray says, 'I will continue to proclaim the truth which is not nullified because some find it hard to believe. I suppose we will always be controversial, but Jesus was too.'

Talking to God

Although the ministry at Rhema was similar to Nicky van der Westhuizen's in its miraculous dimension, it lacked the emphasis on prayer. I found that interesting. God doesn't use a regulation type of person, he is full of diversity. I asked Ray to tell me about his prayer life. For a moment he just looked. In the silence I could almost see his thoughts, then he said, 'All right, I'll tell you. I'm not an intercessor like Nicky, in fact I probably don't spend more than ten minutes a day on my knees.' He continued, 'My prayer life is one of communion with the Holy Spirit. All day long I'm talking to him and the Spirit is talking to me. I'm listening for him in my heart, through the word, through other people, circumstances and even by impressions. My heart is open to the Holy Spirit – the rich communion that I enjoy, is my way of a continuous prayer life.'

Ray usually stays at home every morning until eleven-thirty a.m. That is the time when he's 'in the word', meditating, relaxing and being with his family. First of all he gives himself to prayer and the ministry of the word, only then does he go into the office. Ray certainly doesn't underestimate the necessity of prayer and intercession. He is thankful for those who daily bear him up before the Lord. In the church recognition is given to those whose special ministry is prayer; two people have been appointed to the full time staff for its promotion in every department of the church. There are intercession times, all night prayer meetings, some meet at five a.m., others gather daily or at certain lunchtimes. Alan Burrell has the particular responsibility of teaching prayer and intercession throughout the church.

Sowing and Reaping

The growth in the work at Rhema Bible Church is not attributed first to prayer, as with Yonggi Cho and Nicky, but to the demonstration of the Holy Spirit. Ray said, 'Jesus is seen to be alive in our meetings.' (Nicky had said the same.) And another irrefutable reason, 'I came on the scene at the right time – God's time.'

Ray, just like Nicky, linked the measure of the Holy Spirit's activity with the use of the gifts of the Holy Spirit. The gifts are the means through which his power is demonstrated. If his gifts are limited in their use, so will be the evident power of the Spirit. Ray went further, 'It is essential to teach the gifts of the Holy Spirit. If you do not teach them and honour them they will never be produced and therefore you will never see the power of the Spirit. What you sow in the church you will reap in the church. If the gifts are sown by teaching them, then the benefits coming from the gifts will be reaped.' I latched on to what Ray was saying, it seemed to be the key to so much of what I had seen. What you sow, you will reap. The Bible School sowed expectation and power in the hearts of the zealous young students and they have reaped. Sowing is done by teaching, honouring and expectation, then when the 'seed' has taken root the harvest is certain.

Between my conversations with Ray, I was introduced to practically every aspect of the life of the church. Their spirit of faith and dynamism was a joy to me. The people believed in what they were doing, the message they were preaching and fully expected glorious results. The principle of sowing and reaping seemed to impress me at every turn.

The church has a School of Psalmody – something I'd never met before, it is devoted to teaching praise, worship and music. The school is instrumental in developing the prophetic thrust to the church. It goes almost without saying, because they have sown liberally in this area, they have reaped well. In the meetings they are blessed with excellent musicians and an abundance of mature prophetic song.

The church is pioneering in the area of video ministry. They have not been slow to grasp this new opportunity, by providing video displays for churches and other organisations – their material is out on loan all over the country. In most places the average church service would not make particularly interesting video watching, its activities are far too predictable, but not so with a Rhema church meeting! Ray talked about seeing the power of the Spirit, now thousands watching the videos are having this opportunity; it is shaking churches and groups all over the place. Good Christians are very surprised as they watch God by the Holy Spirit actually coming into a meeting healing people, setting them free from demons, and exposing the secrets of men's hearts. The video and tape ministry is a powerful tool to educate the church.

Giving Place to the Holy Spirit

Although the Wednesday night meeting is primarily to establish the believers in the whole counsel of God, I noted that the preaching time was not given its normal pride of place as in most churches. Usually the singing, praying, reading and worship which take place before the preaching are regarded as preliminaries to prepare the people to receive the preached word. Everything is programmed to dovetail into this pinnacle of the meeting. No so at Rhema: every activity, including the preaching, has a different purpose – to create a climate of faith for the ministry of the Holy Spirit himself. The meeting is governed by obedience to him. The preaching of the word is only one means the Spirit uses to open the people's hearts and prepare the way for his own activity among them. The preachers clearly demonstrate that they regard their contribution as a preparation, by always leaving time for the Holy Spirit to come among the people and meet them supernaturally. So often we can miss this dimension of the Spirit by programming him out. If the preacher continues even when the dinner is burning in the oven, so that the people dash away as soon as he finishes, hurried in spirit, they miss the opportunity of a personal confrontation with the third person of the Trinity.

Frequently as much time is left after the preaching of the word for response and personal ministry as is given to worship and praise before. I believe the word of God becomes far more effective in the people's lives through this simple means of giving time for response. As its challenge is not left unanswered, the congregation become doers of the word and not hearers only. When confronted with truth they respond, by repentance, or possessing new possessions in God; they not only hear the word but receive it, decide upon it, and take action.

It seemed the Holy Spirit endorsed this kind of meeting by coming in powerful demonstration, setting the bound free, healing all manner of sicknesses and establishing people in new gifts and ministries in the Holy Spirit. The Holy Spirit is so attractive, his presence draws people back again and again to the meetings. When he is given free opportunity to move and display his beauty among his people, very little advertising is required, they come running – God is in the place. I'm sure South Africans are no different to those in other nations. The presence of God would revive the most sleepy church and cause those who have never considered Christ, to come, even run, if God were in the place.

Later I sat talking to Ray, and he said, 'Once I was preaching, in full flight and ready to make the next point, when the Holy Spirit said to me, "Get off the platform." I said, "But Lord I'm not finished." Again the Spirit said, "Get off the platform." So in the middle of preaching, I stepped down and as I waited with the congregation, God came – he filled the place with his presence, so that we were all upon our faces.' It had obviously been an awe-inspiring experience. I don't think there are many men who would be able to hear that kind of instruction from the Spirit when they're in the middle of preaching. Ray's heart attitude makes it possible for the Holy Spirit to have control; his ears are open and sensitive to the tiniest whisper from the Spirit.

Co-operating with the Spirit

It was fitting that the last message I heard at 'Rhema' was 'How to co-operate with the Holy Spirit'. Being with the church had made me so much more aware of the third person of the Trinity. I had begun seeing things from a different perspective – it isn't so much what we know, but what he does that counts.

Ray McCauley said, 'We are being blessed and successful here because we are co-operating with the moving of God's Spirit here in South Africa.' As the wave of God's blessing is going across the nation, they want to ride on its crest, along with other like-minded visionary peoples. Free from the clutter of traditions and preconceived ideas, they are willingly being swept along in the wave of the Spirit. Ray McCauley, preaching on co-operating with the Holy Spirit, said, 'Can two walk together unless they be agreed?' (Amos 3:3 KJV). Rhema Bible Church are in total agreement with the way the Spirit is going and as God never changes his ways, they are walking with him.

If we are to co-operate with the third person of the Godhead, our wills have to be set by a conscious decision. That choice is worked out through many different aspects. First of all, by co-operating with the word of God; what God says we submit to and do; we are not hearers only but we're also doers of the word. This is a repeated decision, 'I will do the word of God.' This obedience opens up a new compatibility with the Holy Spirit. We become in tune with him.

Secondly, Ray exhorted the people to co-operate with the Spirit in praise and worship. Again this is an active decision of the will, which releases our spirit to arise and worship God. It is only as the spirit is motivated in this glorious activity, that we really experience true worship. Jesus said,

'The Father seeks those who worship him in spirit and in truth.'

Co-operating with the Spirit means yielding all of oneself to his perfect will. It is impossible for us to miss the will of God if we are co-operating with his Holy Spirit. We automatically flow in God's full will for our lives as we move in his Spirit. Paul said, 'For me to live is Christ', and like Jesus we can say, 'My will is to do the will of him who sent me.' It is an invitation to live in a supernatural realm.

Points to Ponder

- *Have I learnt how to claim God's word so that it changes circumstances and people?*
- *Do I believe God's word as it is written or do I permit unbelief and experience to qualify it?*
- *How can I become more sensitive to the Holy Spirit?*
- *What am I sowing by the words of my own mouth and the attitudes of my heart?*

6: Christian City

Have you got the picture? Nicky van der Westhuizen and Ray McCauley both have churches in Johannesburg on the Rand, the name given to the wealthy, troubled, gold mining area of South Africa and one of the richest places in the whole continent of Africa. Johannesburg is South Africa's largest city with huge industrial concerns employing thousands. The densely populated residential areas offer plenty of scope for hundreds and hundreds of churches. Among the large significant new churches is Christian City in an eastern suburb and as the name suggests, it has a big vision.

Ray McCauley phoned the office at Christian City and made the arrangements for me to visit the founder and leader of this large church, Theo Wolmarans. It is almost as difficult to get an interview with him as it would be to see the Queen of England! He works to a very tight disciplined schedule and is naturally reluctant to give time to unknown visitors.

The office was simple, no surplus money had been spent on facilities – quite the reverse to what I'd expected. The image I had gained of Theo Wolmarans through photographs, newspaper articles and his TV appearances left me wondering how I would react to a successful 'film star' type, but now looking about the office I began to wonder if I had gathered the wrong idea. Their facilities didn't look like an extravagant set up and as Pastor Wolmarans and Christian City are synonymous, I was left questioning.

One of the young pastors collected me and took me on

instructions to Theo's home. He does not work from the office. The car stopped in front of high iron gates, the driver spoke on an intercom and the gates opened for us. Quietly the car slipped up the short drive past immaculate flower beds to the well kept house. A maid opened the door and immediately we were led round the back of the building to a study overlooking the unpretentious garden. A tall, fair, casually dressed young man probably in his thirties, stood inside the patio door and sized me up with his penetrating eyes. After welcoming me, we sat down in a sparsely furnished room, I felt a little like an intruder. I began to explain myself and then he put me at ease by adding, 'I'm seeing you because the Lord told me to see you.'

When Theo completed a year's training at a Bible school in Durban he had plenty of offers for secular employment but didn't know which one to take. As he prayed, the Lord said, 'None of these are for you. You are to give yourself full-time in the ministry.' The same day, his wife Beth confirmed the word God had spoken to him in his heart. The decision was made – no secular employment, he would work for the Lord.

They packed their few belongings into the car and drove to Johannesburg. On September 12th, 1979 he rented a hall in a western district of the city. At the first meeting, the congregation numbered Theo, Beth and two visitors – the following week the two visitors came back with two more. Theo thought, 'One hundred per cent growth in one week isn't too bad.' Eight months later they were 300. A move into a cinema eased the pressure for only a short time – the 400 seats were soon claimed and by July the congregation was 600, standing in the gangways and the foyer. Six months later, only fifteen months from the first meeting, they were 1,500 people. When I was speaking to Theo he said, 'We are now 6,000 people in less than five years.'

Organised by the Spirit

Theo talked in a very matter-of-fact fashion, without a hint of emotion in his voice, although the facts and figures he gave me were amazing. I felt like praising the Lord for his goodness. I found Theo to be one of the most exact and precise people I'd ever spoken to. Like a tightrope walker there was absolutely no question of him being diverted from the path he had chosen. He knew exactly where he was going. Thoughts, aspirations and inspiration had been categorised into goals and programmes. A most methodical man whom I couldn't help but admire. There was a ruthless quality about him, not hard and unfeeling, rather the kind of ruthlessness that Jesus had towards himself when he set his face to go towards Jerusalem. Theo is determined to attain his goals and succeed. I knew I was talking to a very unusual character.

1 Being directed by the Holy Spirit

'There are three reasons why this work has grown the way it has,' Theo continued. 'The first is by *being directed and led by the Holy Spirit.* What happens in this church is what God tells me to do. My life is organised so that God can speak to me.' (That little statement demands reflection.) 'For instance, I prefer to work from this study than from the office.' I looked around the simple room carpeted from wall to wall with a thick, comfortable pile. At one end a large uncluttered desk caught the light from the patio window. A few study books lay open – everything else was neatly filed. Two or three comfortable chairs were the only other furniture, except the occasional table. There was space to walk up and down, or lie flat on the floor in the presence of God. I had the impression a lot of Theo's direction by the Holy Spirit came whilst in that prostrate position. Intimate direction from the Holy Spirit isn't granted to the casual disciple, but is a reward for those who give prime time to listening. What a reward! Theo said he spent two hours in intercession each day, then for his own edification, one and a half hours reading the Bible. When preparing for meetings he would spend a further three hours in study. He said, 'When thousands of people have gathered to hear what God says, I dare not go before them unprepared.' He seemed to carry the mandate for the calling of God in his life with great seriousness. 'That leaves me more or less four hours a day to run the ministry of the church,' he said.

He was very conscious that management and administration swallows up valuable hours. He said, 'It robs the servants of God of their true spiritual effectiveness.' I admired the discipline this man exercised over his own life – especially as he has responsibility for a very large and demanding work. He has made the scriptural injunction to 'devote ourselves to prayer and to the ministry of the word' (Acts 6:4), a pattern for living. So as to ensure the church's administration should not encroach upon his time with God, or be neglected, the running of the church's daily affairs is in the hands of department heads, who in their turn are responsible to Pastor Theo. It is similar to a business organisation.

Theo said, 'Because we are being directed and led by the Holy Spirit, God puts his seal of approval upon the work. Conversions, miracles, healings and deliverances take place week by week. Since the work began, thirty-four people have received their sight, countless deaf have had their ears opened and other amazing miracles take place week by week.'

Periodically Christian City has large healing campaigns, which attract tens of thousands. Hundreds are saved, filled with the Spirit and healed. Theo agreed, the miraculous dimension to the ministry undoubtedly attracts the crowds and has greatly contributed to the growth.

2 Being in the right place

Theo said, 'Secondly Christian City has grown because *I am in the right place*. South Africa is experiencing a gracious, outpouring of the Spirit,' and men like Theo, who are co-operating with the Holy Spirit in this time of reviving are seeing amazing growth. They recognise South Africans are turning to Christ more easily than ten years ago, no one doubts it is supernatural. Ordinary people are hungry to hear the word of God and respond to the invitation for salvation. It is glorious; a sovereign activity, and it is bringing repentance. That's one side of the coin, but on the reverse, God has found some obedient co-workers like Theo, who labour to bring the massive harvest of souls into the kingdom of God. Their open-hearted willingness to obey the Holy Spirit, qualifies them to be channels for God's power. Times of refreshing are spreading upon such a wide front across South Africa, that supernatural manifestations and salvation, would seem almost a predictable occurrence, in any meeting where the Holy Spirit is honoured and given liberty.

3 Doing the right thing

'The third factor to cause our growth is *doing the right thing.* If we are going to see God work, we have to be doers of the word and not hearers only. It is one thing for us to have glorious communion with God, where we share intimate secrets with the Spirit, but the lasting value of that communion is only seen in the fruit it produces.' Theo underlined how essential it is for us to hear what God says and obediently do it. A lot of the direction Theo has received from the Lord, is in the practical details of how to run the church; how to make it more efficient, to build the right kind of fellowship, so that the new believers are carefully nurtured and become effective members of the church. At one time, God said to him, 'You're fishing in the right place but there are huge holes in your nets.' In other words he was having a very effective evangelistic ministry seeing hundreds, even thousands being saved, but they were not being built into the church. The pastoral care was ineffective so the new converts fell away, or in many cases, found other churches.

It was at this time that God directed Theo Wolmarans to establish home church groups, closely modelled upon the pattern of Full Gospel Central Church in Seoul, Korea, where Dr Yonggi Cho now has a congregation nearing the half a million mark. With that staggering example before him, Theo has set his sights and is building. If there is another man who could build a Yonggi Cho-sized church I think it could be Theo! A most determined, inspiring character with an amazing anointing of God upon his life and at thirty-three years old he has got time on his side. The present rate of growth in his church is thirteen per cent per month compound, he told me. He was full of facts and figures. With twenty pastors, only seven of them full time, he is very economical on his use of staff. The church is most carefully organised and administratively scaled down to the bare bones. But to keep abreast with the growth, Theo expects to appoint one new full time member of staff each month.

House Groups

The house group system is of immense importance in Christian City, where Yonggi Cho's teaching on the subject has been faithfully followed. Each home church as Theo calls them, has about twelve people. As the groups gather new members, they are immediately divided in half to grow again. Obviously producing the next layer of leadership is a major task. The full time pastors have responsibility for about 250 people in cell groups, those who are voluntary or part time, care for no more than 100 persons. To assist the pastors in their task there are those who are called area representatives – a man in charge of about six house groups. The lesson material for the weekly group meeting is produced by Theo, who first teaches the house group leaders himself. Careful documentation of all that goes on in the house groups is presented once a week at the teaching class. Any members absent are noted, followed up consistently for five weeks by different persons appointed for the task. If persistent follow-up doesn't bring the straying person back to the church, the pastor himself must visit and then report personally to Theo. With such careful pastoring it appears they've endeavoured to close every hole in the net. The new converts reaped each Sunday, are also invited to be present at the house group leaders meeting. It is their opportunity to see how the house group system works – to personally meet the pastors and be introduced to the home church leader in their area. The system is meticulous and certainly should produce growth.

Future Strategy

As we talked about the moving of the Holy Spirit in South Africa, I asked him for his opinion, 'Is this revival or effective evangelism?' After much thought he said, 'Revival is wisdom to effectively evangelise.' With that understanding of the present move of the Holy Spirit in South Africa, Theo is highly motivated to put his wisdom for evangelism into practice over the next few years. Theo said, 'I consider my first calling in the church to be as a teacher, with an evangelistic ability.' Theo Wolmarans the strategist, has already carefully worked out how he intends to move into an evangelistic ministry across South Africa, with one campaign about every six weeks. Never before have I met somebody who so clearly had thought out every detail, he knew where he was going.

Theo carefully outlined exactly how he plans to become involved in evangelism. 'Before going to a locality I will first identify the people within this present congregation who have some affinity to the area. Out of the group I will identify the ones with the sense of call, those clearly gifted by God and choose from among them, those to be pastors and leaders.' Families prepared to move into the area would also be contacted. Taking this hand picked group of people, he plans to move into the town, rent a large hall or take a tent, for an evangelistic campaign, perhaps lasting one week. Theo said, 'I am sure that by preaching the gospel with the ministry of healing, it will be possible to see four to five thousand people saved during that time.' It sounds easy on paper, but as we talked it was obvious Theo had thought out every contingency and clearly expected success.

Through evangelism he intends to establish churches, although he said, 'I have no desire to plant anything that would afterwards be linked to myself or form a denomination. I want to see totally indigenous local churches, but I would endeavour to help them grow by every manner of assistance.'

Once the campaign is finished Theo plans to send teachers into the area to conduct Christian Growth seminars for all the converts. By holding the group together he hopes to securely ground them in the word of God and to impart a vision for ongoing evangelism through the church. Theo said, 'I will choose the pastor and leaders, then after they have set up home churches, I would consider the work has become an independent church.' Theo's analytical mind had carefully covered every conceivable problem. He had all the answers at his fingertips and although it appeared he was ready to go, he said this was the strategy for the following year.

Teaching How to Build

The major burden on Theo's heart concerned the churches. He longed to see them firmly established with the new converts won through effective evangelism, growing up into mature Christians. As he said, 'Revival is wisdom to effectively evangelise.' God is pouring out his Spirit – by co-operation with him, hard work and a church building strategy, the revival fires will spread all across the nation.

Theo began to share other plans he has for helping to produce strong churches. He was organising his first national church growth seminar, when he planned to invite ministers from all churches. He intended to teach them the methods and organisation found to be successful at Christian City. The first subject would be his approach to church administration, which is quite a departure from traditional ways of thinking. His sights are set on huge churches being established, having congregations in tens of thousands. To handle this size of operation effectively requires a business-like approach so the seminars will cover subjects like:

– purchasing land
– building
– administration
– dealing with staff and finances
– how to relate to the media
– how to advertise
– how to buy and sell
– how to market books, tapes and videos

Apart from this list of topics, the more traditional subjects of evangelistic methods and the essential place of the Holy Spirit in all church building activities, would not be neglected. The seminars promise to be very practical, will help to give substance to dreams, and raise the level of faith in all the participants. Hopefully denominational ministers, as well as small fellowship pastors from every state in South Africa will attend.

Dedication and Enthusiasm

Exactly one hour later, from the moment I'd walked through the door, the same young pastor who had escorted me to Theo's home appeared just outside the study. Theo took note of his presence, stood up, the interview was over. As we walked towards the door Theo said, 'I cannot change my lifestyle. I have to know the power of the Spirit and the anointing of God upon my life. People come in their thousands to hear me and expect miracles. I can't go before the people unprepared.' Obviously this intense young man with amazing abilities, feels the weight of responsibility upon his shoulders. His response is a carefully disciplined and dedicated life. We shook hands and I left, he did smile and I admired what I'd glimpsed of an unusual man.

Larne Hugo, the young pastor in charge of the music ministry of the church talked on the way back to the church complex. 'What did you think of Theo? I tell you he's a stickler for punctuality. If he says be there at three o'clock, you'd better be there.' We drove into the large, thirty-three acre site where in 1982 an auditorium providing seating for 3,000 was constructed, financed by various loans. I was told the congregation in April '84 numbered 8,000 attending one of three Sunday services.

Two Sundays later I walked into the beautiful auditorium again, to enjoy one of their Sunday meetings. The building was at most, half filled for the ten-thirty meeting but the praise and worship was a delight and sensitively led by the musicians. Unfortunately Theo didn't preach as he had just returned from a visit to the United States, but after the ministry of the word from Bill Price, in common with practically all the churches I visited in South Africa, there was a time for response. About a dozen people desiring to be saved walked forward, the sick were prayed for, and demons cast out. As I was leaving some enthusiastic British immigrants told me how they had come to South Africa, been converted, filled with the Holy Spirit and had their lives totally changed. 'Is there anything like this happening in England?' they said.

The ministry from the church continues all through the week, in the Bible School and Christian Growth Seminars. It is interesting to note the kind of subjects which these churches, moving in the power of the Spirit, consider are basic essentials for the new believer. Whereas the emphasis for teaching new believers in most traditional churches would be becoming a church member, breaking of bread and perhaps water baptism, the subjects covered in these 'present truth' churches are surprisingly different.

- Righteousness – one's right standing as a gift from God
- Water baptism
- How to claim your healing
- How to minister healing to others
- How to take your authority as a believer over demons, problems and circumstances
- How to exercise faith
- How to pray
- How to meditate in God's word
- The Holy Spirit
- How to receive the Holy Spirit
- How to recognise the voice of God
- The coming of the Lord and the Rapture.

It becomes evident looking at such a list, the teaching aim of the church is to produce Christians capable of ministering to others and confident to exercise faith on their behalf and for themselves. Again I thought of the Scripture, 'Whatever a man sows, that he will also reap.'

7: Jesus Alive in Durban

Already I had been thrilled by the evidence of the powerful moving of God's Spirit in South Africa. The large churches I had visited exercised a wide influence across the country. None of them were local churches in the strict sense of the word, but each had a national vision and a compulsive missionary zeal which knew no bounds. The cassette tape, video and book ministries from these churches alone influenced thousands and thousands of people. The national television and radio networks frequently invited their leaders on to the programmes so that these men's names were becoming widely respected as those whom God was using. I prepared to leave for Durban where I was to meet Dr Fred Roberts of the Durban Christian Centre, another key man in what God is doing in South Africa.

First Class Students

I was met at the airport by a young man called Neville and his wife Rina, with their two children. Neville had been a pastor at the Hatfield Baptist Church but was restless, longing to experience a greater measure of God's power upon his life. As he sought God, the opportunity came for him to go to the Bible School at the Durban Christian Centre. This meant selling their home, moving to Durban and trusting God to provide for themselves and their two children. Repeatedly, whilst in South Africa, I was challenged by the whole-hearted commitment of many students in the various Bible schools. To attend, they had to find the money for their fees, their daily needs, and for a large number of students like Neville – enough to keep their families also. The whole experience became an adventure of faith.

Chatting over a cup of tea I realised that Neville and Rina were no ordinary Bible school students, but people with outstanding faith and ability, in God's school of preparation for a future effective ministry. Most weekends Neville has opportunity to preach in one of the hundreds of churches in the area. The weekend before I arrived he had believed God for at least one complete miracle to take place in the meeting on the Sunday evening. Boldly he called those with incurable diseases to come forward and a woman with a skin condition like a septic acne all over her body walked forward. Neville prayed for her, immediately the skin on her arms changed before their eyes and healing spread all over her body. A most unpleasant condition totally disappeared. The Spirit who works miracles was making his presence known.

In 1979 in an area called Kurulman, in the north-west Cape, Neville saw another notable miracle happen. A man was present in the meeting with a leg so swollen that it was about the size of his waist, gangrenous, pitted and full of deep holes. The man's life was in danger and his leg was to be immediately amputated. The strange condition had been caused by the bite of a poisonous spider and aggravated through working with asbestos. The sick man had resisted the doctor's advice to have the leg amputated because God had told him, in six weeks time he would be healed. During the meeting, Neville went up to this man, as he sat in his chair and said, 'Get up and walk.' Miraculously the man got up, stood and shouted, then ran all around the place as his leg shrank back to its normal size, shouting at the top of his voice 'He's alive, He's alive, He's alive.' It was exactly six weeks to the day. God had kept his appointment and Neville who was expecting miracles became part of the planned intention of God.

This was my first introduction to Durban Christian

Centre and I thought to myself, 'If this is one of the Bible school students, what is the church going to be like?'

The Sunday Meetings

On Sunday morning I was bubbling with excitement as I anticipated gathering with the church to praise and worship. What was God going to do? We went to a very large cinema in the centre of Durban. Although the neighbouring streets were quiet with the shops closed, people were streaming from the car parks and buses into the cinema. The congregation was really mixed. Whites, Indians and Africans, people sat anywhere, although the Indians tended to sit in a block, thus expressing their naturally insular character.

After a time of worship and praise led by Pastor Fred's wife, Nel, the whole congregation participated in the breaking of bread. Although the congregation was very large, there was a good friendly atmosphere. About one hundred people responded when the question was asked, 'Who is here for the first time?' As the communion things were gathered up Pastor Fred Roberts spoke out a word of knowledge about pain in the body. Crowds of people came forward and Fred began to pray for them. He quickly walked down the line of people lightly touching them and they fell down under the power of the Spirit. Each person was caught and lain on the floor. There were little children and even very old people. A deaf woman heard immediately, she gave testimony and praised God.

Another woman, who three weeks previously had told a tragic story, came again in the healing line, she wanted further prayer. She had been involved in a major accident where her hips and pelvis had been crushed. After many operations she was partly paralysed and in constant pain, unable to walk without the aid of crutches. For one year and seven months she had dragged herself round in this condition. That previous Sunday God had immediately healed her; she testified that she had walked without crutches for three weeks, but had come again for a complete healing. One of her shoes was built up three and a half centimetres and her gait was still ungainly. We all rejoiced in what God had done so far and looked for a total restoration. Fred prayed again, and the short leg grew immediately so that she was no longer able to wear her uneven shoes. She beamed with joy as she walked up and down unsupported and bare footed. She appeared to walk awkwardly although her legs were obviously the same length. As she went to walk away Fred called her back and again prayed for her. He said, 'This hip still needs some healing.' He lifted his heart to God for total restoration, for the power of God to come upon her and put everything right. Immediately she fell down as the Spirit came upon her but after a few moments, was up rejoicing, confident that the work God had so beautifully begun, would be totally completed. When those healed during the morning meeting were asked to stand to testify, at least forty people were on their feet.

Fred encouraged the people to believe the word of God by his own testimony. A short while ago he had a growth in his ear and the medical advice was that it should be immediately removed. It was extremely serious. But he said, 'God had spoken to me and encouraged me to believe the word of God, "By his stripes I was healed." I continued praying, believing and confessing the word of God. One day great faith rose up in my heart. The growth appeared to become detached and I was able to pull it right out of my ear. When I returned to the doctor and he looked, he said, "That was very nice surgery!" The ear was completely healed.'

Pastor Fred Roberts then preached from Colossians 1:25 about the mystery of Christ within us. He only spoke for about thirty minutes and nothing he said was new, but every word came home to my heart with unusual impact. He said, 'Under the old covenant only certain people were anointed with the power of God for a specific purpose, but now in this dispensation we not only have the Spirit with us but in us. The tabernacle in the Old Testament was built for God, a place for him to dwell, but in this dispensation we have become that habitation.' Pastor Roberts then began to talk of the shekinah glory and the presence of God filling the uncovered tabernacle in the wilderness. I wrote in my notes 'hatless' for it seemed to be an apt description for the uncovered dwelling place of God. Suddenly I was so conscious of God's presence as Pastor Roberts spoke of our bodies being like an open temple for God to fill with his presence. The message ended acknowledging the anointing that abides. We were instructed to cultivate the inner small voice and to co-operate so that the Spirit flows through us. His ministry contained the same emphasis that I'd met before, of positively speaking the Scripture, proclaiming and receiving its truth. By this means the mind is renewed by the word of God, and attitudes are changed.

Always an Invitation

It was hardly a gospel message but immediately an invitation was given to receive Christ. As I listened to Pastor Roberts drawing in the net, I recognised the expertise of the evangelist. He gave the invitation in a positive way, saying, 'You will respond,' and other such expressions. All over the large auditorium people began to raise their hands. About fifty people walked to the front, then through a word of knowledge, 'There are four people in this area who should respond,' he pointed to a certain row. Immediately four people stood up and walked to the front. I was amazed at the response. It seemed the people must have come wanting to be saved. Some standing at the front were in tears, broken with conviction of sin, there were Indians, coloureds, whites, a cross section of all communities. Counsellors knelt with them as they repented, believed, confessed and prayed.

A genuine open thankfulness for the new converts was immediately expressed. They were called 'the precious ones, God has given us'. There seemed to be no limit to the appreciation Pastor Roberts and the congregation expressed for the converts. There was an immediate flow of love towards them. People came and shook them by the hands, hugged them, prayed for them, and thanked God openly as I had seen at Rhema in Johannesburg. It seemed so warm and loving in comparison to a typical stoic British response.

In Durban Christian Centre, they have about three hundred converts each month. The ministry of counselling goes on continuously. They are visited, brought into beginners' classes then eventually established in house groups.

The Beginnings

Once the meeting was over I was gathered up by Nel and taken with them to lunch. Fred began to talk a little about the work and I asked him about himself. For many years he'd been a pastor of a Full Gospel Pentecostal church working in a Durban suburb. During that time God began to speak to him and in 1956, after a period of restlessness, he went to San Diego in the United States, where he was exposed to the power of the Spirit in a new way. After six months God told him to go back to South Africa and to open a centre for all people regardless of race or colour. Whilst still pastoring the pentecostal church, he began evangelistic meetings in the centre of Durban. He longed to reach the 90,000 people who live in the city. During the latter part of the 1970s, small groups of people from various churches were meeting, seeking to be baptised in the Holy Spirit.

Dr James van Zyl and his wife Meg met Fred and invited him to come to Stanger, about fifty miles north of Durban, and so began his relationship with this interesting couple. For eight months he taught a small charismatic group gathered in their home. At the time he happily went there, although looking back, now wonders how he put so much effort into such a small group when he was so busy. The group, mainly Afrikaners from the Dutch Reformed Church, were baptised in the Holy Spirit and then in water. Strain developed between Fred and his denomination when he resisted the intention to put a pentecostal pastor in charge at Stanger. Fred recognised God was doing a totally new thing and he feared it would be stifled by traditional pentecostalism. His own attitude made him realise that he was beginning to walk in a different direction.

James van Zyl began to move out into a healing ministry, so working together with Fred they continued hiring halls on Sunday afternoons in the centre of Durban. In no time two thousand people had committed their lives to Christ. The dilemma for Fred between the evangelistic ministry and pastoring the small church in the suburbs became intolerable. Eventually he left his denomination. When they announced they were going to start a church in the centre of the city, two hundred and fifty people came for the first meeting. The second week they had five hundred. Fred said, 'I was doing nothing, only opening the doors and putting on the lights. God was let loose among the people.' It was the year 1979 when this burst upon the scene.

When Nel and Fred had offered to take me for lunch I was unaware that Fred had been fasting for more than twenty days. He makes it his custom to fast for prolonged periods every so often. Before the work was launched in 1979 he sought God in a forty day fast. Now I understood why something of that shekinah glory, of which Fred preached, had touched the lives of the congregation that morning. As I enjoyed my rice and curry, Fred feasted, breaking his fast with a little fruit.

Building with New Plans

Pastor Roberts sees himself primarily as an evangelist; but

since the success of the rapidly growing Durban Christian Centre, he has turned his thoughts and efforts to making Durban Christian Centre a secure church that establishes the converts, produces mature leadership and continuously grows. Now free from denominational strictures, he is being taught by the Spirit and shown new ways of building and organising the church.

Fred went on to say, 'South Africa has a history of powerful movements of God's Spirit. In the early part of this century some of the great men of the Elim and Assemblies of God, as well as American pentecostal churches, were powerfully used in South Africa. Thousands were swept into the kingdom through their miraculous ministries. They left an indelible mark upon the history of the church. So that, to this day, there are three large pentecostal denominations in South Africa besides countless pentecostal movements amongst the different black communities.

Along with other denominations, the pentecostal churches have been jolted by the charismatic renewal and are now openly reaching out to some of the new independent churches. At first they were suspicious of the 'faith men' but attitudes have been softened and greatly influenced by the ministry of Reinhard Bonnke and Nicky van der Westhuizen, two men whom God is using nationwide and who have pentecostal backgrounds. Fred then went on to say, 'But now there appear to be three camps within the country. The restoration camp, the faith camp, and the charismatic camp, although the edges are being blurred in the power of what God is doing here in South Africa. Through the outpouring of the Spirit we are seeing a powerful evangelistic move across this nation, accompanied by signs and wonders. At the same time God continually brings men from all over the world who share their insights about the establishing of the church.' Fred's open, receiving attitude has made it possible for them to be exposed to some of the finest ministry – its diversity has blessed them.

The vision for a multi-racial church is still clearly in focus. They have a coloured and Indian pastor among the leadership, who especially deal with their own communities. Because of the structure of each society in South Africa with communities living separately, each developing its own ethos, it becomes difficult for those of another community to readily communicate, especially when it comes to pastoral matters.

Each day trains bring the workers from their townships into the city of Durban. The half an hour journey is turned into a golden opportunity for declaring the gospel. Outspoken black workers distribute Gospels, others sing and praise God and lead many to the Lord. Their teaching and preaching during the journey is seeing a continuous harvest. I somehow couldn't quite imagine such happenings on our inter-city trains in England.

No opportunities for witness and evangelising are lost. Durban is a very large holiday resort with beautiful beaches. The weather is idyllic, most of the year the resort offers hot sands and sunshine to South Africa's holiday-makers and a growing number of international visitors. In 1983 and 1984 the church organised a 'Jesus Convention' in a beautiful building only a few steps from the beach. The daily meeting drew hundreds and hundreds of people who were thrilled at the miracles they saw, then heard the gospel and were saved.

A Bible School in a Cinema

The following day I had an opportunity to go and see the Bible school in progress. As we went into the converted Lyric cinema suddenly my thoughts were far away! On the opposite side of the road is an Indian spice factory, the smell pervading the air reminded me of mouth-watering curry. The smell was so strong, I thought someone must be cooking nearby. Pushing such delightful anticipation away, I went up the steps.

The Lyric cinema is used only for the Bible school, and not for Sunday worship – it is far too small. The school began in 1981 with forty students. With a two year cyclic programme and material drawn from Christ for the Nations at Dallas, Texas, they cover a wide range of subjects. Most students do one year training which is considered sufficient for the average person wishing to go into ministry. There are also correspondence and part-time students as well as an audio cassette and video section. The students are of all ages, backgrounds and multi-racial.

In the same premises they operate a telephone ministry where they receive about twenty-five calls a day. It is a demanding task, counselling desperate people, seeing many saved. I asked the reasons for the rapid growth, depth and variety of ministry that had grown up through Fred Roberts' work in Durban. I was taken into the video lending library and the bookshop and there I found videos of men of God from all around the world. Here was an answer – they are not exclusive, but open to hear from God through a wide variety of men. Guest speakers are invited to minister in the church on a Sunday night and then for three days in the Bible school. This exposes the students to a wider breadth of vision and they can appreciate the expertise of different men of God. Although Fred may not fully endorse the emphasis of some, he does not necessarily refuse their teaching.

Fred Roberts is one of the few men in South Africa who has been able to visit the Full Gospel Church in Seoul, Korea. Yonngi Cho's method for bringing stability to a large church through the house group system influenced Fred Roberts. With three hundred or so people responding to the gospel each month they are battling with ways of seeing these enquirers turned into committed members. Special classes are organised but at present only about twenty per cent pass through the class and eventually get built into the church. Cell groups meet each week in the various localities and because so many members live a long distance from the centre of Durban, a variety of meetings are held in the different localities.

Through aggressive evangelism and powerful gifts of the Spirit, almost any church would grow, but Fred Roberts underlined another principal reason for growth. He said, 'God showed me I must release all the ministry he has placed in the church.' This was one of the lessons he learned from Yonngi Cho in South Korea. Those gifted by the Lord are put to work, the ministry gifts distributed in the body are utilised, no exception is made for women, whose valuable contribution is encouraged and received.

It is evident that a man with a personal life of prayer and intercession like Fred Roberts, is going to see this ministry evolve within his own church. Besides gathering weekly for prayer, three months were set apart for special intercession against the demonic stronghold of Hindu and Muslim spirits which rule over Durban. Everywhere I went in South Africa I met a spiritual awareness among Christians that one of the major enemies to the gospel, is the phenomenal spread of the Muslim faith. Some were openly fearful of the powerful influence of Muslim spirits—Christians aware of the danger are getting together to pray. In Durban, with a two-edged sword, they attack the foe by prayer and evangelism and are seeing fruit.

As I pushed my belongings into my suitcase back at Rina and Neville's house, and prepared to move on, I thanked God for the church. Thanks welled up in my heart for Pastor Fred Roberts, and the vision he had stirred in dozens of young people in the Bible school. Thanks for lives touched with fire and now dispersing all over the country, starting churches, gathering together the hundreds of people who are being saved, and those joining the staff of other large growing churches. As the work in Durban expands, Fred I am sure will have the joy of some of his home-grown leaders, choice students, joining him as co-workers, and what better choice could they make?

8: Medicine That Works

The stories I had heard about Dr James van Zyl intrigued me. Rina, my hostess willingly drove me to Stanger to meet him, an hour's journey north of Durban. Tall sugar cane grew in the fields alongside the road; glimpses of beautiful beaches and blue sea invitingly appeared between folds in the hills, as we left the fun holiday city of Durban.

Stanger is a small town where approximately eighty per cent of the population are Asians. The car turned into the shopping area. I looked up at the imposing mosque on the hill and then at a Hindu temple on the corner. We drove along the main street; yes, there was a familiarity, it looked a little like India where I had lived for many years, but hadn't the same feel. I wondered to myself, 'What's the missing ingredient?' Then it dawned on me, there were so few people, and very little traffic; so different to the main street in any small town in India, where people, animals, smells, noise, clutter and colour vie with each other for attention.

James and his wife Meg live in a pleasant house, with their youngest child, a twelve-year-old son, and Meg's mother. For twenty-one years Dr van Zyl was the district surgeon in Stanger and also held the honoured position of mayor for five years. Like most South Africans he was a church-goer, a member of the Dutch Reformed Church. In his unconverted days, he said, 'I was an influential worldly person, like others, mainly concerned with having a good life and making money.'

Attracting His Attention

So often one of the most direct ways in which God deals with his people is through financial matters. Dr van Zyl came to a crunch point in his new Christian life when he was developing a block of flats on some land he owned near to the sea front. In good faith he had borrowed a huge sum of money to get the construction going but suddenly it looked as if the deal was going to fall through. Bankruptcy stared him in the face. He cried to God, 'If you get me out of this one, I will really serve you.' God heard that prayer. Without having to make any requests, he was offered loans, even from individuals. All was not lost; the flats were completed, every rand paid back and a bonus blessing landed in James's lap. A remaining scrap of land was purchased by a developer and James received the proceeds from the sale of another four flats. God doesn't do things by halves. James was steered out of a successful secular life into an abundant spiritual ministry. Through pressure upon his finances God secured his attention and then blessed him in every way.

Dr James van Zyl decided to give up everything and follow the Lord. He resigned as district surgeon and withdrew from political life. At the time it was a huge step of faith, but he said, 'I knew God as my Father and was convinced he would provide for me and the family. I felt confident that he would love and intimately care for us in every way, just as a father cares for his own children.' He added, 'The salary I now have is only a quarter of what I used to earn, but it goes further and I've always enough.' James said, 'The rich young ruler walked away from Jesus with a sad countenance, but when Jesus spoke to me, I took up his offer.'

Dr van Zyl is renowned for his remarkable healing ministry which began in such a small way. He could have missed everything God purposed for him, if he hadn't been scrupulously obedient to the little promptings of the Holy

Spirit, that launched him into praying for the sick. After all, he was a medical doctor and his methods of dealing with the sick were not normally praying.

At this time he was introduced to an amazing video of A. A. Allen, an American with an incredible healing ministry. The sights he saw gripped James so that he watched it again and again. All kinds of sicknesses were healed before his eyes, the cripples walked, deaf heard, totally paralysed people rose from their beds, and the blind saw. A desperate longing came in James's heart for the gift of healing in his own surgery.

Launching Out

One day God stepped in. An eighty-year-old, blind African came into the surgery, led by his son, who said, 'Will you pray for my father?' James stood forward and examined the man's eyes. There were cataracts in both of them. James told the man he could arrange for surgery, but as he spoke the Lord said in James's heart, 'Pray for this man.' James asked, 'If I pray for you do you believe Jesus can heal?' and the man said, 'Yes.' James prayed, the man immediately saw, but through a misty haze. The cataracts had gone and the man went away. That evening James was thinking, 'I know it happened, a blind man saw! But I've no way of contacting him, I don't even know his name, he just came and went.' Somehow it seemed like a dream.

The next day another man, elderly, blind and led by his son came into the surgery. He too had cataracts. It was like a re-run of events from the day before. Again the Lord spoke to James, 'Pray for him.' Immediately he prayed and immediately the man was healed! This time Dr van Zyl wanted to take a note of the man's name, he didn't keep records of these poor, welfare patients in his free surgery. Joseph Kumala took his medical card from his pocket and James wrote, 'A blind man now healed of cataracts.' He handed the card back to the old man and the next patient walked in.

Six weeks later a line of African men patients were walking past James's desk in the surgery and the Spirit said to James, 'Call that man, the one with the walking stick, and pray for him, do not send him for medical help.' The poor man, in severe pain, hobbled over to the doctor. James prayed for him and the man was immediately healed. When he took the patient's medical card he was astounded – his name was Joseph Kumala. What about his eyes? Excited, James carefully examined them – there wasn't a sign of cataracts, his sight was perfect and his severe back pain had vanished.

Through implicit obedience to the prompting of the Spirit, Dr James van Zyl was launched into a ministry of healing. When God spoke to him, he acted, prayed and God healed.

Preach the Gospel and Heal the Sick

Fred Roberts from Durban was overjoyed at this amazing development and they decided to arrange joint meetings, where Fred preached and they both prayed for the sick. At one of their first meetings a man came forward with severe pain, he had lung cancer. It was a long-standing problem. Most of one lung had already been removed, he also suffered with a heart problem, was a smoker, an alcoholic and only kept alive with masses of drugs. After being prayed for, the man went to his home, but during the night suffered the most excruciating pain. The following day it became so severe that he thought he was having a heart attack, and was admitted to the local hospital where they did various medical tests; all proved to be absolutely clear. Next they X-rayed his chest and discovered that the area where the lung had been removed was filling up with a brand new lung! The Jewish doctor who brought in the X-rays was shaking, he couldn't believe his eyes; holding them up he compared them with the old ones. Although the man had previously been treated for heart disease, now the doctors could find no evidence of it, even the scarring had gone. The man was totally healed. Dr James van Zyl worked closely with Fred Roberts for a number of years until their ministries grew to the point where both of them had many others working with them.

James is an Afrikaner, so understands how to minister in an acceptable way to his own people. Quietly spoken, he prays for the sick, rarely raising his voice. With his wife, he established an organisation called Christian Centre from which his healing ministry, mainly to Afrikaners, touches the whole nation and speaks into the spiritual vacuum surrounding the Dutch Reformed Churches.

South Africans have a great respect for training and education. A minister of the Dutch Reformed Church undertakes seven years of training which affords him an equal status in society with a medical doctor. When Dr James van Zyl, a respected medical man, links his knowledge with simple faith in the word of God, the traditional Afrikaner feels secure enough to trust him. Because he is a doctor, they more readily believe in and accept the powerful demonstration of miraculous healings. James doesn't disturb them by being a fiery preacher, that isn't his style. In a fairly matter-of-fact fashion, he explains to his congregation that they can be healed through the Lord Jesus Christ. He explains the gospel and calls people to receive Jesus as their Lord and Saviour, then prays for the sick. The gifts of healing and miracles are his prime ministry.

Raising the Dead

I settled back into the comfy chair as Granny handed us coffee whilst she lovingly chided the dogs for getting in the way. James continued to speak calmly of his ministry and without any hint of emotion, talked of occasions when he had seen the dead raised to life.

Dr van Zyl told me of an instance when he visited an

Apostolic Faith Mission Church in Secunda, an industrial area where petrol is manufactured from coal. He said, with feeling, 'The new industry, and its way of life, had instigated a decline in old moral values which were soon replaced with the wicked activities associated with wine, women, and song.' His meetings were advertised and attracted the sick and needy. One evening, as he made the invitation for those who wished to receive Christ, among the people walking to the front was a man with extremely severe asthma. While stepping forward he fell down dead in the aisle. James van Zyl went and examined the body, and said, 'The signs by which any medical man would determine death are present.' Immediately he called the spirit of death out of the man, who shook and came back to life – yet died again. A second time James called the spirit of death out, commanding him to go and leave the man. Again the man shook and came back. This happened four times. Eventually the spirit of death left – the man got up, walked and was healed.

'I've seen God raise the dead other times too,' James went on. 'At a place called Warmbaths an elderly woman died sitting in her seat, while I was preaching. Everybody was turning, looking, talking and I could see a commotion was beginning – I wondered what had happened. Stepping from the platform, I walked over and saw the old lady was dead. I commanded the spirit of death to come out of her; she shook herself, stood up and was perfectly well. God raised the elderly woman, not because the elderly shouldn't die, but as a sign to the unbelievers to provoke faith.'

I am telling you this story exactly as Dr van Zyl told me. I felt absolutely amazed at the things I was hearing. Looking round the very lived-in sitting room, everything was so ordinary and down to earth, yet the events he spoke about were extraordinary, though mixed up with the commonplace affairs of life.

Perfecting the Gift

James holds evangelistic healing missions at the invitation of various churches and groups for about one week in each month. Using large halls or church premises he preaches the gospel for six nights, especially teaching how the gospel is linked with healing, so as to bring the people to faith. He then prays for the sick and demonstrates God's power to heal.

God had brought Dr James van Zyl to a special level of faith concerning certain sicknesses. For example, he is convinced that God will immediately heal those with back and ear problems, also cancers. His own faith is being extended all the time; a year ago he came to a new position in faith for blind eyes. His faith is indomitable concerning God's ability to heal all and everything, but step-by-step a finer quality of faith is being purified in him and exercised over particular diseases. I met others in South Africa who spoke in the same manner – they too had attained a place of faith, which gave them a commanding authority over certain sicknesses and conditions.

An elderly lady came to James's and Meg's home, she was blind and wanted to see. With Mark 11:23 on her lips and in her heart, this seventy-five-year-old woman believed she would receive her sight. 'Truly I say to you, whoever *says* to this mountain, "Be taken up and cast into the sea," and does not doubt in his heart, but believes that what he *says* will come to pass, it will be done for him.' Dr van Zyl prayed for her. Fifteen minutes later, sitting, chatting and having a cup of coffee, she suddenly said, 'I can see.' At first her sight was vague and misty. Later, while sitting next to her daughter-in-law in the car on the 300 mile journey home, she asked, 'What are those white marks on the road?' When told it was paint to mark the centre of the road, she said, 'I never knew they painted roads.' The following day she could read the fine print in her Bible. Dr van Zyl said, 'Many people come to the home, they travel from far distances, even foreign countries. These are not sceptics, they've made a personal effort to come, and ninety per cent are instantly healed. Miracles are an everyday affair in our lives.'

Apart from those who are healed in the public meetings, hundreds are also converted. Dr van Zyl said, 'About ten per cent of those responding to the gospel in our meetings go on with the Lord and are established in churches.'

When is a Miracle a Miracle?

'A miracle is instantaneous, I'd call it divine healing when it's delayed,' said Dr van Zyl. 'Let me give you another example, in one of my meetings a Dutch Reformed minister came bringing a family of deaf and dumb people. There was the mother, father and one child. When I prayed for them the minister couldn't help but laugh for joy, then it turned to crying and sobbing as he saw this little group talking fluently and hearing one another – that's a miracle!'

'And I can tell you another story,' said James. 'You know in every meeting there are a few sceptics, watching to see what you're going to do. Besides the sceptics, there are honest folk who need to be convinced that God really does heal. A group of Christian youth workers were present in one of my meetings: because they want entrance into many different kinds of churches, they were inclined to qualify healing, by saying, "It's not really the will of God to heal everybody," although God's word says plainly, "Pray for one another that you may be healed." I looked at this group of young people and called the youngest two to come forward so that they could see exactly what was going to happen. First of all, they saw a leg grow, I had them stand close and watch as the leg grew to match the other: but that wasn't all, a young man stepped forward and showed me his arms. One appeared to be a lot shorter than the other. I said to him, "Don't fool with me or with God." The young man took off his coat and I could see his deformity was genuine.

Whilst doing military service on the Angolan border, he had been shot in the shoulder so that the joint was mangled, making his arm about five or six inches shorter. I prayed. The arm grew, four, five, then six inches. Just straight down. The bones, muscles, ligaments of the shoulder were completely reconstructed. The young man jumped up and down as if shot out of the gun himself. He shouted and started running round the room, then took off his shoes and threw them as hard and as far as he could across the hall! I said to him, "Why are you doing that?" and he said, "I longed to play cricket but this shoulder has stopped me from throwing a ball, now I can bowl again!" There was no need to try and convince the youngsters any longer. God does miracles.'

Praying for the Sick

Dr James van Zyl is absolutely childlike in faith. He questions nothing and believes everything. I was staggered at the capacity of this very intelligent man to just believe. 'When you pray for the sick, I notice you always cast out the spirit first. Why do you do that?' I asked him. James said, 'My only formula for praying for the sick is in Mark 16 and verses 17 and 18, "These signs will accompany those who believe. In my name they will cast out demons, they will speak with new tongues, they will pick up serpents and if they drink any deadly thing it will not hurt them, and if they lay their hands on the sick, they will recover." As I read those few verses,' James said, 'it seemed to me that if the signs are to follow, we must first cast out the spirits; so I come against the spirit of the particular sickness, if it's stubborn, I'll pray in tongues, then I'll lay my hands on the person and pray. I do it this way because it works.'

'My medical training,' said Dr van Zyl, 'tells me the things I see happen, can only be of God. Other men like Nicky van der Westhuizen and Ray McCauley are not capable of diagnosing the diseases, so perhaps they do not recognise how amazing are some of the healings. When God reconstructed that young man's shoulder, I could imagine the miracle God was doing inside. Every part was put back in its right place, refashioned in shape and size and caused to function again perfectly. What a miracle! I still have confidence in medicine, I believe it to be God given. Medical people are healing the sick. I know some people consider it to be spiritual to come out of the surgery, after the doctor has told them they've got cancer, saying, they don't receive it. Now I feel it's unwise to go to a doctor and then not to receive what he says. The best attitude is to go, hear what he says, face the problem squarely and then believe God. Don't trust the doctors more than God.'

'Everybody wants a miracle, but sometimes God doesn't work that way and the healing comes in stages. There are times when the person prayed for seems to become worse rather than better. We need to understand the ways of God and persevere in faith.' And then James gave an illustration from ordinary life. 'If you have a chronic appendicitis you're not terribly ill. Occasionally you may have niggly pain, but it's bearable, although there'll come the point when you decide to go to the hospital and have your appendix removed. After the operation you are perhaps one of the most ill people in the hospital. You can't laugh or cough, and barely move, but you know the offending part has been removed, you are healed although you feel ten times worse. You went in well and now you feel ill. It is not uncommon for divine healing to follow a similar course.'

'I now have great faith to pray for cancer,' said Dr van Zyl, 'I invite the sufferers forward, pray for them and some are immediately healed while others walk away with divine healing working in their bodies. God doesn't have any stereotyped ways of healing. A lady doctor, Salome Betcher, from Pretoria, had terminal cancer. The treatment she received had made her hair fall out, her skin hung loose on her bony body. Humanly speaking she only had one or two weeks to live. With her last spark of life she went to Tulsa,

USA, to a Christian hospital, where she saw many Christian doctors helping such hopeless cases as herself. They were praying in tongues for those dying with cancer and many were healed. Medically no treatment could reverse Salome's condition, but as she stayed in the hospital she was totally healed. Now she has grown a new head of hair, 'it is beautiful, thick, and quite unlike her own hair before the disease.' What a lovely bonus!

Near to Cape Town there is an important university called Stellenbosch. It is one of the theological establishments in South Africa which train ministers for the Dutch Reformed Church, with their own strong emphasis on knowledge and tradition. Few are to be found there with faith like a little child. James came to this seat of learning to hold a series of meetings. Many lecturers and learned folk were seated wondering what they were going to hear. Among the group was a minister of the Dutch Reformed Church, suffering with cancer. Dr van Zyl had no special way to pray in front of this rather special audience, he commanded the angel of death to leave the minister, then the spirit of cancer to go in the name of Jesus. The man was instantly healed and began to speak in tongues. Consternation spread among the learned group of people. What did this mean? Why did the Lord cause him to speak in tongues as well as heal him? I think the Lord must have a sense of humour!

Life for the Traditional

Dr van Zyl had story after story to tell, each amazing and only one of very many that could be told. God had given him wide acceptance with the Afrikaners. They could have been left outside of the move of the Spirit, because their predictable religious lives would naturally never encounter this 'acts of the apostles' style christianity. But God has given Dr van Zyl a remarkable entrance among the non-pentecostal Afrikaans churches, wherever he plans meetings, they come in large numbers.

At Ventersdorp he had a very successful campaign where seven ministers from local churches came and two of them got saved in one week. The tent was filled night after night and many of the people converted were baptised in the swimming pool during the week.

At another place about 500 people packed the town hall. A local lawyer led the singing, but the people didn't know how to praise God and it was awful. The poor singing didn't deter the people who crammed in, even filling the centre gangway of the hall, leaving hardly any room to move. After everyone was seated, the local postmaster, a high school teacher and two others came in carrying a man on a bed over the heads of the crowd. Dr van Zyl had looked out across the congregation and had wondered how he would call the people forward to pray for them. There was only one tiny space left, six foot by three foot next to him on the platform. The four carrying the man, made for that patch which disappeared as they lowered the stretcher. Dr van Zyl took a quick look; there on the stretcher was a man in the most desperate condition. He was covered up except for one bony hand lying on the sheet, and an arm which looked like a stick, the bones only thinly covered by skin. He had no energy whatsoever, even to lift his hand or head. His wife sat next to him and occasionally dribbled water into his mouth. Dr van Zyl turned his eyes away, he hardly wanted to look.

James stood up and spoke, but there at his feet on the platform in front of all the people was the man. Every eye in the place was riveted upon him, all wondered what the doctor would do. He could almost feel the question coming back at him, 'Can you heal this man?' He went on to say, 'You can imagine how I felt, I was asking myself, have I got faith to speak to this sickness? I knew it was a cancer. First of all I began to pray for people with back troubles, then those with hearing defects and one by one everything else. People were being saved all over the place, they began to shout and praise God. He was healing them, suddenly there came a sense of wonder at what he was doing. Then I heard a weak little voice saying, "Pray for me, pray for me." The man on the bed was calling out and I knew the time had come to command the sickness off him. I prayed with the authority of Jesus, commanding the cancer to leave him, and walked away while he still lay on the bed. The man said, "Now I can get up!" The words just came out of his mouth involuntarily rather than him saying them. He shocked himself. He sat up, swung his legs over the edge of the stage and stood up. He was healed. All the people were shouting and praising God. When power comes down and God does wonders, even the most traditional, formal, religious people, shout and praise God.'

You Get What You Ask For

Mrs Blyde Steinberg, a young mother, who lives at Springs in the Transvaal, had heard Dr James van Zyl on television and when she learned that he was to visit Springs, she determined to be at the meetings. Mrs Steinberg suffered with multiple sclerosis. Both arms and legs were paralysed and she was completely blind. Blyde had twin girls, whom she'd never seen. Encouraged by James's miraculous ministry, she cried out to God, 'Oh Lord, if you would only heal me, just one of my eyes and just one arm, I would be happy.' During the meeting many people were prayed for and healed. Then James prayed for her. Immediately she regained sight in one eye, and movement in one arm. She rejoiced and rejoiced, thanking God and said, 'Now I'll go home and see my children.' The following day she was back thanking Dr van Zyl, who was curious about the limited extent of her healing, then she told him how she had prayed. James told her to go home, repent of limiting God, and believe him for total healing. This remarkable young mother had an obedient heart. She went home praising and worshipping God and believed she would be completely healed.

Nine months later, Fritz Kemp, the minister of the church she attended, encouraged the people to praise God by clapping their hands. As Blyde Steinberg endeavoured to clap her mobile hand with her paralysed one, she was spontaneously healed. Both eyes, both legs, both arms, her whole body received strength – praise had set her free. She clapped and clapped her hands then walked straight out of her wheelchair to the piano where she sat and miraculously played in the Spirit. What a mighty God!

A Telephone Connection to Power

Many people who have never been in one of Dr James van Zyl's meetings, find that he is the person they wish to contact when confronted with a desperate situation. Their confidence in his ministry has grown through his appearances on television or they have heard him on the radio. The media has made it possible for him to influence tens of thousands of individuals.

Tragedy entered the lives of a young professional couple; the mother was a pathologist and the father, a dentist. They lived in Pretoria. One dreadful day they were very grateful that Dr van Zyl was at the other end of a telephone; their little six-month-old baby girl fell into boiling water – it was a minute or so before she was rescued. The distraught parents, crying to God, telephoned James asking him to come immediately to Pretoria. It would have taken at least six hours to drive there; instead he prayed for the child over the telephone, believing God to make her whole. She was admitted to hospital with virtually no hope. Her entire skin had been removed, with second and third degree burns nearly all over her body. The natural prognosis was imminent death from renal failure.

The poor little baby was totally bandaged from head to toe. A week later she was still alive and it was decided that some of the bandages should be removed and an attempt made to do skin grafting. The child was taken to the operating theatre but while they were preparing the instruments, a special scalpel blade broke as it was placed in its handle. Another was used, that also broke, then a third one was inserted and that too broke! With no further sterile blades available, the child was sent back to the ward. The following week, the baby remarkably alive despite the dreadful prognosis, was taken again to the operating theatre. On this occasion they ran out of time and were unable to complete the list – so the child was left. Two weeks had gone by. The third week she came again to the theatre, they carefully removed all the bandages and wonder of wonders, the skin underneath was totally whole.

Growing Legs

For some reason plenty of scepticism surrounds the miracle of legs lengthening in answer to prayer. It is regarded with caution, like a circus trick, perhaps because it looks so easy. I have seen legs grow to the correct length in a matter of moments, so that built-up shoes could no longer be worn. It's quite spectacular.

Small discrepancies in the leg lengths are frequently discovered in those who suffer with back pain. The person is made to sit in a chair with their legs straight out in front of them and by matching the heels, the legs are measured for length. If one leg is found to be shorter than the other, it is usually considered to be the culprit causing back pain. Praying for the offending short leg usually brings immediate relief.

One thousand letters flooded through the letter-box in Stanger – one day's response to a radio programme. Besides the letters there were countless 'phone calls, one from a young girl who said her mother was in absolute agony, not able to move, because she had severe back pain. It took some time but eventually the mother was seated next to the telephone and James instructed the girl how to measure her mother's legs. Then she said, 'Yes one is shorter than the other – the right one is shorter.' 'I will pray,' said Dr James van Zyl. Holding the telephone receiver in one hand and placing the other upon her mother's legs she joined James in prayer and shrieked as the leg grew whilst she watched. The woman stood up, healed and so thankful to be free from pain.

On another occasion the wife of the minister of a Dutch Reformed Church telephoned Dr van Zyl because her husband was in severe pain. They lived in Georgetown. The poor man couldn't sit on a chair but his wife laid him on the floor next to the telephone and following Dr van Zyl's instructions, she measured her husband's legs and discovered one leg two inches shorter than the other. Dr van Zyl was hundreds of miles away but as he prayed the leg grew. The amazed couple stood up and praised God – the healed man was able to walk around without pain or a limp.

Not by Might, nor by Power, but by My Spirit

We finished our coffee, the 'phone rang and James left the room. I didn't move for a while, I was lost in my own thoughts. Dr James van Zyl is a quiet, slightly contemplative, down-to-earth sort of person. He enjoys getting his hands dirty, mending things and even more, inventing things. His special love is growing orchids; he retreats into the orchid house to be alone with God. If it isn't orchids it's fishing. When Meg and James return after a week of meetings, James can't wait to get down to the sea. He pushes out the boat and is off – a fishing trip in the small hours of the morning, what could be better! Sitting alone out in the middle of the calm balmy sea, who knows what fellowship he enjoys. Being alone appears to be part of James's pleasure and recuperation, before standing once again before the sick and needy. Part of the fun of a fishing trip is the good food it provides for the table; that evening we all enjoyed fresh fish and the freezer was well stocked too. From my experience with meeting other men whom God was using in outstanding miraculous ways, I realised there was no one particular type. God seems to delight in variety.

Granny walked into the sitting room. 'She's the one who prays for us, look, our prayer warrior,' Meg said. For her age Granny was the most vital, active woman you could imagine. She was never idle, busying herself with household jobs and overflowing with loving care for everyone who walked in the house. Although Granny was well into her eighties she was exceptionally young at heart, even coping with the intricacies of two-way radio – the son-in-law's latest toy. Her ageless spirit was so well developed, you felt you were dealing with a young woman. She easily communicated with her married grand-daughters who visited with their babies and when it came to the time for me to leave, she hopped in the car and drove me to my friends.

The following day I visited the office where on average a thousand letters a week are received in response to the newsletter they send out. It contains stories of testimonies of healings, teaching and articles to encourage faith in the Lord Jesus for salvation and for healing. The newsletter is aimed at stirring up prayer for the work, their mailing list runs into tens of thousands. All across the country there are those who faithfully intercede for Dr James van Zyl and he would be the first to admit that the ministry which flows from him is largely dependent upon the prayers of the saints. Granny praying continuously at home adds her prayers to those of the intercessors and workers at the office and book shop. Their authoritative praying has cleared the way for a flow of God's miracle working power.

Recently the work has moved into a new home, a large building has been erected to house every aspect of the ministry including a place for the church that has been established in Stanger. Contractors put up the main shell of the building but all the internal finishing work was done by the fellowship, Dr van Zyl himself doing most of the plumbing.

All the ministry will now be gathered under this one roof, including their publishing work. In the past very little literature has been produced in Afrikaans to proclaim the gospel or teach healing. The Christian Centre in Stanger has made a major contribution in this area. A large number of booklets have been written, compiled or translated from the English, to spread the message of faith, healing and salvation. They are sold all over the country.

As I was driving away from the new Christian Centre building I was introduced to David Llanga and Clement, two Zulu brothers leading an assembly among their own people. They were collecting supplies of literature. The blessings flowing from Dr van Zyl's ministry spill over into all the different communities, his spoken ministry as well as tapes and books strengthen many churches. Among the Christians I always observed open loving relationships between the different races. Separate works exist because the people live in separate areas, speak different languages and their cultures are very foreign to one another.

Miracles Communicate

Unexplained miraculous happenings are familiar to Africans – they are the mighty tool of the witchdoctors, who hold whole communities in the grip of fear. Their authority is beaten into the people through fear and endorsed by supernatural acts and power. Unfortunately over past centuries the church has stood by like a powerless onlooker at the convincing works of darkness, performed by witch-doctors, but today, the Holy Spirit is sweeping across South Africa. The amazing ministry which seems almost effortlessly to flow from Dr James van Zyl is only a part of the mighty thing God is doing all over the country. Hundreds of un-named people, from all races, are moving in these supernatural dimensions. God has seen fit to open up a way for his power to be displayed in terms that people understand. The church is becoming a channel for the power of the Almighty God. God is almighty, his power greater than any demonic activity, even the most outstanding displays from witchdoctors. As in the days of the Acts of the Apostles, the gospel is being preached with signs following, miracles happen, the crowds follow and many are saved.

The ministry of men like Dr van Zyl functions like bait, attracting crowds in thousands. But a crowd doesn't make a church and the painful task of building new converts into viable, stable, caring churches is the major challenge in this new move of the Holy Spirit. What a small difficulty compared with the major tragedy of no power and no growth. Praise God the gift of miracles is being restored to the church!

Points to Ponder

- *Could the Holy Spirit lead me into a new ministry? Am I sufficiently aware of his voice?*
- *How much does my intellect stand in the way of simple faith?*
- *What would have to change in my life before I could receive an anointing for power?*

9: Is Small Beautiful?

Wherever the Holy Spirit is at work he is doing the will of the Father. In these last days before Jesus comes again, God is intent upon restoring his church to its former glory. So much of its initial power and life has been lost over years of apostacy. The resurgence of spiritual gifts and power in the church is evidence that God is reversing that situation and bringing the church into a new dimension of effectiveness.

Whilst some concentrate on power, others are more concerned with the structure of the church. As they see the Spirit of God moving in South Africa their efforts are concentrated on building relationships within the churches, forming good house groups, having the right kind of church life which will gather converts and keep them. When thousands of people respond to the gospel in large meetings their major concern is, how are they going to be built into the churches? The evangelist sees the people respond but the churches are often inadequate at following up enquirers and building the new converts into the body of Christ.

Whilst driving along the road away from Johannesburg the Lord began to speak to me. The landscape was barren and dry with scrub and odd bushes here and there. The countryside was monotonously the same for mile after mile and then as I turned a bend in the road, suddenly my eye was drawn to a group of very large trees; a welcome sight. They cast deep shade across the road and the noise of the wind in the high branches was refreshing and lovely. I looked into the shadow underneath the trees – a swift flowing river glinted in the patches of sunshine. Big trees grow where there's plenty of water. Everything they needed for healthy vigorous growth was provided by the fast-flowing river running in the little valley.

The Lord said to me, 'Those big trees are not adequate in themselves to cover this whole landscape, the small bushes are as essential as the big trees.' I then understood the Lord wanted to show me what he was doing among his 'little bushes'.

Wherever the Spirit of God moves, a spontaneous growth comes in the church. All over South Africa new churches and fellowships are springing up, often without any denominational allegiance. It is a new phenomenon as widespread as the country is wide. When rain pours upon dry, thirsty land, seeds germinate and plants appear, it seems like a miracle. That's what has happened in South Africa, the rain of the Spirit is wetting the very dry and barren land and life is springing up. Throughout the country, God is putting his hand upon individuals, who with an exuberant faith are doing things they've never done before. New believers, those freshly baptised in the Holy Spirit and hungry for more, seek out like fellowship. The groups are often small, but in the climate of what God is doing, they hold a mighty potential for growth.

Variety but Unity

The majority of new fellowships have started since 1979. Out of the hundreds I could have visited, I chose a representative few. In East London I met the leaders of four different churches; one a Baptist, two were from different Pentecostal denominations and the fourth one an independent fellowship, yet they all had a number of things in common. All were experiencing growth, taught the necessity of the baptism in the Holy Spirit, met in house groups, and were reaching out to other Christians in the town to express the unity of the body of Christ. Two of them had building programmes for a 2,000-seat church planned on opposite sides of the town. Although they were small compared with the huge churches I'd already visited, they obviously had no intention of staying small.

I discovered that men leading smaller works were more inclined to comment on other movements in the country. A lot of things are happening of which they are not part. For instance, Piers Steenekamp identified two major influences from the United States – 'the restoration, discipling school', and what he called, the 'faith input', from men like Kenneth Hagin, Kenneth Copeland and Jerry Saville. Another young pastor, Leon van Rooyen, said the charismatic movement brought revival to the traditional church whereas the Rhema ministry has stirred up the pentecostals. The restoration movement is beginning to have some influence, especially among smaller fellowships; and could be considered a revival of small home groups and sound church structures. Leon said, 'They have a valuable contribution to make to the foundational needs of the church. Each of these influences in South Africa has brought new life,' Leon said, 'but any one of them that puts a lid on itself and walls around and becomes exclusive, will fall into the denominational trap.'

Is it Revival?

Size and growth speaks success. Understandably smaller groups and especially those whose numbers are static, spoke from their insecurity, naturally threatened by mighty ministries hitting the headlines and huge crowds flocking to meetings. Despite a little resistance to 'American influences' they couldn't disguise their admiration for what one man called, 'very anointed ministries'. The importance of these 'very anointed ministries' has become so widespread that even small indigenous fellowships bear the marks of their influence, by being more prepared to pray for the sick, and use the gifts of the Spirit. According to their faith, they have varying degrees of success.

It is quite interesting how views of revival are coloured by one's own personal experience. I never found one man involved in the small work who would say that South Africa was experiencing revival, although with one voice they said, they lived in anticipation. A Baptist pastor said, 'I'm confident God is going to do something wonderful. At present we're in a cycle of blessing, our growth is a result of the last wave of renewal.'

Wherever one goes in South Africa the Christians are talking about revival, whether they think they're experiencing it or not. It's one of the hot subjects. The signs, wonders and miraculous displays of power turn thoughts automatically in that direction. Even among many of the smaller churches where these manifestations are uncommon, it does not hinder them from recognising the genuine moving of God's Spirit. Small churches in South Africa are certainly more open to manifestations of the Holy Spirit than many of their counterparts in Britain; mainly because their minds are not sterilised by an atmosphere of cynicism and unbelief, so prevalent in other western countries.

South Africa is a vast country and people are well accustomed to travelling very long distances. Quite readily the local respectable denominational pastor will go a thousand miles to where no one knows him, and be present in meetings which he might consider unseemly, if they occurred in his own church.

Peter, such a man visited Hatfield Baptist Church in Pretoria, where Jim Spillman from the United States was preaching. Jim said, 'Do you believe in the Holy Spirit?' and then he blew – 250 people fell over as the power of the Spirit came upon them. Peter said, 'I saw it with my own eyes, then Jim Spillman, the most anointed man I've ever seen, called all the pastors together to pray for them. I made up my mind I was not going to fall down, just because everybody else did, but as he spoke, the Spirit of God fell upon us and it was impossible to stand on my feet.' This unexplainable experience, tucked into Peter's memory, coloured his attitudes towards the moving of God's Spirit, although it did not appear to give him any expectation that God could do it for him. Peter had never seen anything miraculous happen in his own church, but now he had good reason to be open to the Holy Spirit, although he didn't understand his ways of working.

Different Faces of Restoration

A clearly defined grouping of smaller churches are those introducing the principles of restoration taught by ministries from the United States and England. Derek Crumpton among others, is recognised for his apostolic ministry to a number of these small groups. Their emphasis is upon relationships but I gathered by speaking to many different leaders, their expectation from these relationships differed very widely. One pastor who wanted apostolic help in his church said, 'I really would appreciate a spiritual father, who is secure enough not to manipulate me or use and control me.' The open-heartedness of many South Africans makes them very welcoming to ministry from all over the world, but different men repeated the same apprehension, 'Yes we are open to teaching and apostolic wisdom from overseas, but not for authority from overseas.'

Many of the smaller churches I visited defended their size by pointing the finger at the large ones and repeating, 'Yes, crowds are saved on Sunday but they're out the back door on Monday.' Unfortunately even small churches didn't appear to be immune from the same disease. One I visited experienced expansion in 1981, but since that time about 100 of those added have drifted away and for the past two years the church has been static at about 600 members, although it grows 'by thirty people per month!'

In another city I visited a number of flourishing smaller groups. They had established clear leadership, trans-local relationships and house groups, with the aid of apostles. Although they were unique churches with their own character, their leaders were being influenced by the atmosphere of faith within the whole church of South Africa. Their openness to signs and wonders and powerful demonstration of the Spirit gave them the potential to be fast growing, secure churches. In a few years time they may prove they possess a few solutions to prevent the leakage of new converts back into the world.

In the natural there is a huge variety among bushes; not all have the same potential size and rates of growth differ vastly. The same pertains for churches, where size is not the only measure of success. Some of the smaller churches I visited were abundantly successful in the community where God had placed them. Churches are modelled upon the abilities of the leader. Many good pastors can only handle about 150 people; vast crowds and efficient church organisation are not their scene. Obviously some churches would always be small, but others, from their very inception, were destined to grow because they contained the seeds of something huge. Faith was in evidence even if the fruit of their faith was not yet visible, only time was needed.

Sowing Mustard Seeds

One Sunday morning in Cape Town I visited a new church obviously growing from a very lively seed. I stood back and watched as the red truck backed up on to the cinema steps. Before Neville MacDonald, the driver, hopped from his seat, two young men were heaving the speakers and sound equipment into the cinema. They had arrived for the Sunday morning meeting. Neville and his wife Wendy came to Cape Town only eight months previously to start a church. Groomed by his father-in-law, Fred Roberts in Durban, he hired the cinema, put an advertisement in the local paper and began to preach and pray for the sick. Eight months later, the congregation numbered 400 each Sunday evening and about 200 in the mornings. Weekly, people were being saved and the converts trained in classes; a young and vigorous work, planted in faith and already bringing forth a good harvest.

Neville and Wendy had had the privilege of one year at a Bible school in the United States before working for a few years with Fred Roberts. Their gifts were well developed, Neville a careful teacher and conscientious in all the work of the ministry. Wendy is no stranger to the spiritual world and understands how to take advantage of every opportunity for extending the work of God. I was confident that her clear perception would be a valuable early warning system to detect the wiles of the evil one as he attempts to oppose this new work. Neville and Wendy are good partners in the work, with God's calling clearly written upon their lives. I have a suspicion that in a few years this church may well be numbered among some of the larger ones in South Africa.

Observing the spiritual state of the church in South Africa is like walking round the garden in spring-time. Everywhere you look something new is popping up. Certain plants hold the promise of being small and beautiful, others large and spreading. There is a right place for a multitude of smaller fellowships throughout the country – like ground cover in the garden. Looking to the future, I would expect them to have impaired viability, unless they constantly stir up faith and live in the same quality of life that is motivating the expanding churches. That is a difficult task with a small work, where sameness can lead to its fossilisation.

10: Bringing the New out of the Old

My journey to Bloemfontein brought me into contact with 'a vigorous plant' that I'm certain is destined to become large and spreading: again it began with a high dose of faith. Johnny and Ann Bossman are Afrikaners; people whose families have lived in the Bloemfontein district for fifty years and belonged to the Apostolic Faith Mission, the largest pentecostal church in South Africa.

For many years Johnny, with his wife and family, pastored an AFM church in Bloemfontein. A restlessness came into him and for a short time he left the area and pastored another AFM church, in the East Rand. He had grown up in the strait-jacket of pentecostal denominational ways, but somehow, they began to chafe. By 1978 he was feeling so unsettled, that with his wife and family, he left to go to the United States to see what he could learn. The visit became the turning point of their lives.

The Bossmans tended to think that Americans were extravagant talkers, braggers, out to impress and very unreal. This attitude naturally made them cautious and slow to receive – but the more they travelled and the more they saw, they realised they had made some wrong judgments. These Americans were not only big talkers, they were big doers, very positive in their thinking, full of expectation and always talking success. Johnny said, 'They never talked small.' That visit made a deep impression upon them; Johnny continued, 'It transformed my whole attitude. I seemed to wake up, and receive a new ministry.'

Pastor Bossman and his wife are not inexperienced youngsters, impressionable and easily swayed by new ideas; no – they are serious-minded, godly people with a long experience in the ministry. The visit to the USA brought them to a crossroad in their lives. Johnny didn't need to be told, they would never fit back into their old mould. Their hearts had been expanded, their vision broadened, their expectation had reached a new level. Past dreams came into focus as possible realities. Thoroughly shaken up, straightened out, turned around and put into a new way, they returned again to South Africa, two new people.

Starting Again

They resigned from their denomination, returned to Bloemfontein and prepared to begin again from nothing to build a church. The decision was made, and an advertisement went into the local paper announcing their first meeting. As Pastor Bossman looked out across the 400 people who came, he knew that many were just curious to see what was going on. He had no illusions, there was a long way to go before a church would be built.

When I visited Bloemfontein the church had been established for only one year. Johnny said to me, 'If I had known what was going to happen, I would have grabbed twelve men, shut the door and trained them in leadership for three months, before doing anything else. This past year has been absolutely hectic. We now have 400 people committed to this work, we carefully taught commitment because we want to see the church built in this place.'

The temperature was minus two degrees the day I arrived in Bloemfontein and it continues to scrape around that level during the winter months in the Orange Free State. They hit endless difficulties in finding a permanent meeting place and now the only cold comfort they can offer to their congregation of 450–500 people who meet with them each

Sunday, is a tent, a sobering test for any believer's commitment on a winter's day.

Dr van Zyl had told me that through the ministry of Johnny Bossman, a blind minister of the Dutch Reformed Church in Pietermaritzburg had received his sight; so I was interested to know, if the work at Bloemfontein had been established through the miraculous. Pastor Bossman said, 'Through my visit to the United States, I've come to a new understanding of the work and ministry of the Holy Spirit. No one specific aspect of the Holy Spirit is responsible for what is happening here; the restoration of praise and worship, and the gifts of the Spirit emphasising the miraculous have all been taught as a total package to the people. The Spirit himself is the irresistible drawing power.' Many people had received healing, but Johnny's expectation was for so much more. He said, 'We have been experiencing the power of God in spectacular, supernatural ways. The Spirit of God has fallen upon groups of people, baptising them all in the Holy Spirit at once, or delivering them simultaneously from evil spirits. These things are new for most of our people: they have come from Dutch Reformed, Roman Catholic, Baptist and Presbyterian backgrounds. We're walking a new path together, the veil of tradition is being taken away. The people were like the blind, following, but without knowledge of the power of God.'

This infant group of believers is growing up fast and strong. They have declared war on the powers of darkness ruling over Bloemfontein, a headquarters for Satan-worship in South Africa. Systematically they have been binding the powers of the strong man and believing God will give them the victory again and again.

Pastor Bossman has now gathered a group of fine leaders. Like others involved in new works, they approach the challenges ahead with reverent holy fear, conscious that they have not walked this way before. With no past experience to help, they are cast upon the Spirit of God for direction and wisdom. Unfortunately such fine attitudes can soon diminish as the ministry becomes expert and professional. Praise God, this group of leaders still in the first flush of their new life, excited with what God is doing, and thrilled to be part of it, were very open and teachable. Sobered by their previous experience of ineffective Christian work, they didn't want to make the same mistakes again. Hungrily they talked of their desire to see God restore his purposes and power to his church. They wanted to be co-workers with him and were thrilled at the vision God was setting before them. Although at present the work is quite small and young, it had been planted in faith and mixed with the vital ingredients of expectancy, vision, determination and zeal. It will grow.

The Power of Worship

Pastor Bossman described a vision he had had, which came like a little preview of what God intends to do. He saw himself standing on some high ground looking at a crowd of people. They were worshipping, absolutely lost in worship and at the same time gently moving closer together. Instinctively he knew they were coming into the Body of Christ. Their worship seemed to create a cloud, like a huge mushroom over the company of people. The more they worshipped, the larger it became. From his vantage point in the vision, he looked beyond the edge of the cloud, where he could see women with hats, handbags and Bibles, men in their Sunday suits, all hurrying towards the gathering people. Instantaneously he knew they were symbolic of the traditional religious people of South Africa – running and rushing towards the vast area of worship. As they joined the throng, they too worshipped. The area enlarged, and the cloud stretching out to cover them all, extended continuously as they worshipped.

With his attention still riveted to this impressive worshipping crowd, Johnny then noticed miraculous happenings taking place among them. Nobody was praying for the people, but they were being healed by being in the presence of the worship. Again his eyes strayed to the far edges of the large white cloud and he wondered, 'Why are the people streaming in?' He could see they were church-goers, he questioned, 'Why are they coming?' and the Lord said to him, 'These are the denominational people who want to praise and worship in Spirit and in truth, they're hindered by the traditions and the strictures of their denominations.' As he watched he knew the expanding cloud of worship and praise would reach a point when it would burst. Then people from all over the nation would gather and enjoy the benefits of the gifts of the Spirit, which would provoke further multiplication into an endless stream to the whole of South Africa.

Looking at this amazing vision, Johnny knew that he had a part in it to play and was confident God would direct him. An indelible impression was stamped upon Johnny's spirit. Praise and worship is the predominant key to the release of God's purpose in South Africa.

Seeing Churches Grow

Church growth organisations abound in the United States. In-depth investigations have left no stone unturned in the quest to find the secret to church growth. Volumes have been written on the subject and coast-to-coast seminars expound various formulas guaranteed to cause your church to grow. No doubt the message they proclaim is one the church desperately needs to hear. Too long it has lived in smallness. Yonggi Cho threw down the gauntlet and many Americans ran to pick it up.

During his stay in the United States, Pastor Bossman was greatly influenced by various teachers on church growth. He said, 'In most denominational churches, the pastor is paid to do the work and the people watch him do it – a system totally counter-productive to growth.' Johnny

Bossman said, 'One of the keys for growth is to get the people working.' Now in South Africa that is not going to be an easy thing to do. It will need an earthquake to bring a change!

Pastor Bossman gleaned methods of church growth from many churches, organisations and individuals including Dr Robert Schuller. As a member of Church Growth International, whose president is Dr Paul Yonggi Cho, Dr Schuller's methods are greatly influenced by those which have been successful in South Korea. After mustering all his information, Johnny said the Lord gave him a plan to adapt this teaching for South Africa. He set up The Institute for Church Growth in South Africa and runs seminars to train leadership throughout the church. Among other subjects, he teaches how an efficient church requires the right people to be in the right place. The one-man ministry of the past can never fulfil the purposes of God. In the business world, each person does the work most suited for them; in the church the right person is there for every task, so we must find them. The children of darkness are wiser than the children of light. The world knows how to do things efficiently and produce results, surely the church can learn.

My visit to Bloemfontein became rather special. I had intended going on a certain Friday but the Lord spoke to me very clearly and told me to go two days earlier. On the plane whilst travelling, he told me to read Haggai chapter two, and to share it with the group when I arrived in Bloemfontein. I wasn't sure how that would be possible but waited to see what the Lord was going to do. The opportunity came and first of all I spoke to Pastor Bossman himself who became most excited when I told him what God had said. Immediately he called everybody from all the offices to come and listen. Unknown to me they were in the middle of a battle of faith, trusting God to meet a large financial need. The evening before and again in their morning prayer time together, God had spoken to them from the same passage of Scripture, assuring them that he was going to meet their need. You can imagine they were delighted and amazed as I shared the word of God. It came as confirmation that God would supply their every need, including the immediate financial one. After praying and prophesying everyone scattered back to their offices and I was alone again with Pastor Bossman. Within a few moments the door burst open and with great excitement the secretary announced, 'The money has come!' What a joy it was to witness God's faithfulness.

The work, just one year old, began in faith, and continues in faith. While it follows that path, it is guaranteed to be fruitful. Those who believe shall not be put to shame.

It Costs to Follow the Lord

How desperate are you to see the power of God upon your life, in your church, and in the nation? The more I travelled and the more people I met, so the conviction grew – it costs to follow the Lord.

During my time at Reinhard Bonnke's Crusade in Cape Town I had frequently noticed a man with a light upon his face, who appeared to be bearing a lot of responsibilities for the local support of the crusade. Opportunity came for me to be introduced to Walter Snyaman, the leading pastor of a church called The Lighthouse. I kept hearing that name from all sides, as many of the helpers on the site were members of The Lighthouse; a converted theatre in a prime position in town, used for the church, a coffee shop, restaurant and bookshop. During the crusade they provided office premises for the follow-up work.

Walter Snyaman welcomed me into his office at The Lighthouse. I immediately liked him, a very sincere and open person who bore the marks in his character of one who had been tried in the fire. Pastor Snyaman had been a member of the Pentecostal Protestant Kirk, the second largest Afrikaner pentecostal movement in South Africa.

The same church that Nicky van der Westhuizen had belonged to.

Up until 1976 Walter Snyaman had been quite content leading a successful church in Cape Town. When the charismatic renewal began to revolutionise many of the denominational churches, especially the anglicans in Cape Town, somehow he thought it didn't seem quite tidy having the pentecostal experience outside the pentecostal church! That same year he went to the United States and his testimony is the same as Johnny Bossman's. He came back a totally changed man.

The End of Legalism

Walter Snyaman said, 'I was brought up in the Afrikaner pentecostal way of judging and condemning. Everything was law. Everything was judged by its outward appearance – how the women dressed, their hats, whether they wore jewellery or not, certainly women shouldn't have bare legs or wear trousers, and men should wear smart suits and ties. All judgments were on the outward appearance. A man was not considered to be spiritual if he turned up in a jumper and no tie!' The visit to the United States tore Walter Snyaman's attitudes to shreds. He was shocked to find God moving in such powerful ways through people whom he would never have considered qualified by his standards. Whilst he was a wistful observer, he said to himself, 'I want what they've got, but I don't want to look like them! I was so upright but so wrong.'

He returned home to South Africa, to the same PPK church in Cape Town. He began to seek God for his future; he was changed and didn't feel at ease in his old situation. The legalism had been shaken out of him and the demonstration of power through men of faith had unsettled him.

At this crucial time, Walter Snyaman had a visit from a man with a prophetic ministry. His word came as confirmation for the guidance Walter felt God was giving. The church was prospering under his leadership and there was need for them to move out of their cramped church buildings. The word from the prophet seemed to seal the move into the theatre, now called The Lighthouse.

Those involved in the new surge of the Holy Spirit immediately find themselves out of step with Christian brothers and sisters with whom they had worked quite happily before. Walter Snyaman's life had had a radical shake-up and because he is a truthful person, he could not deny the vision God had given but had to follow it. God was calling him to something bigger, and wanted to demonstrate the power of the Spirit among his people; the Lord would use Walter Snyaman in ways not possible in the past. Tensions grew, the new wine was not sitting comfortably in the old wineskin; the move into The Lighthouse unintentionally became a move out of the denomination. Suddenly the local church were confronted with big decisions, the majority willingly moved on with their pastor into a new spiritual arena.

Commitment is Expensive

The people proved their commitment to the new work by amazing sacrificial giving. 200,000 Rand was needed to buy The Lighthouse building, refurbish and make it suitable for a Christian meeting place. When they'd given all their money, they continued to give jewellery, antiques, electrical goods, their hi-fi systems, furniture, anything that could be sold, till every rand needed was paid.

Walter Snyaman, an experienced gifted, middle-aged, pentecostal pastor, who had known a good measure of success in his previous churches, has moved into a new gear. What was accomplished in the past now pales in comparison to the aspirations of his heart and the vision stamped upon his spirit. Before he could become part of the new move of the Spirit in South Africa he had to experience the painful surgery of being separated from his legalism. It seems that no group is immune from slipping into traditional legalistic ways. Truths revealed in the light of the Spirit, lose their attractiveness and powerful cutting edge, once they are regulated by organisations, rules and regulations.

The new building will seat about 2,500 in the main auditorium, but they have a long way to go; at present about 1,000 members are committed to the work, which is mainly reaching the white community. They are growing by leaps and bounds, and most encouraged since Nicky van der Westhuizen came to The Lighthouse to hold a campaign. The place was crammed and 400 people had to stand on the pavements outside, unable to get in. Miracles took place, people were saved, and demons fled when commanded in the name of Jesus. The kingdom of God has come in a new wave of the Spirit which of necessity must leave the old behind.

11: The Black Majority

Whenever I asked about the work of God in Africa I was always told, 'Oh! You should talk to David Newington.' I am very grateful that I stopped off to meet this fascinating man, with an exceptional knowledge of Africa. David Newington founder and director of Emmanuel Press in White River said, 'South Africa is a unique place, a polyglot of communities which still today, includes those from the Stone Age to the jet age.' David continued, 'There are nine official languages here and the scope for the gospel is endless. In recent times the charismatic movement has swept very powerfully through this country, especially among the Anglican churches. South Africa has always been an extremely religious place; the Afrikaners are by tradition, God-fearing, Bible-believing people – it is virgin soil for the work of the Holy Spirit. The pentecostal message and the charismatic movement began among the whites but has long since spilled over into all black communities.' David went on to say, 'Yes, this is revival. More people are being saved pro rata here, than in a dozen European countries. Something new is happening and now breaking through into a more radical movement.' David said, judging from every evidence that he has in the office at Emmanuel Press, where they daily receive ten to fifteen thousand letters, revival is sweeping across South Africa, and going on into other African countries. 'What is drawing the hundreds of thousands of people to hear the gospel at Reinhard Bonnke's crusades and other such big evangelistic outreaches across this huge continent? – nothing less than a powerful move of the Holy Spirit. It is revival, but everything in God gets bigger.'

David has been in Africa for about forty years and is almost an institution himself. He spoke with careful conviction out of the vast resources of his knowledge of this huge continent. 'God is doing something new and very powerful.' David emphasised that as the Spirit of God is poured out in greater intensity upon the nation, he expects the morality of the nation, and of individuals, to be challenged by the pure holiness of the Spirit.

In the most gracious manner David honoured the work that is being done through the Rhema churches, recognising that they are one of the means by which God is bringing revival into South Africa, but he expressed a reservation. 'If the revival is to gain momentum and really bring a challenge to morality, sacrifice needs to be preached.' He said, 'The life of Christ is woven in sacrifice and shall the servant be above the master? The message of the cross which may appear somewhat old-fashioned to today's Christian, and the inherent teaching of sacrificial living, is essential. These will further the work of revival in South Africa.'

Most of the churches I had visited were predominantly white, either English or Afrikaner, but every one of them was open to any race or colour. The political strictures in South Africa hinder people of different races worshipping together but do not forbid it. The simple fact that blacks and whites do not live in the same locality, obviously divides the people up.

South African Tribes

David Newington, with his intimate knowledge of Africa said, 'There are four and a half million white people in South Africa, almost three and a half million coloureds and Asians, and nearly seventeen million blacks, a conglomeration of different tribes. Over the centuries four distinct groups of Africans (the Hottentots, the Nylotics, the Negroids and the Bushmen), moved southwards into the melting pot of South Africa and evolved into distinct tribes. The Bantu is the collective name given to the mixture of these once separate peoples who have now become established in Southern Africa. The historic mixing-up of the groups has not destroyed the strong tribal differences. The blacks of South Africa are a very diverse group of people with different languages. In comparison Nigeria, a far larger country, has only two separate languages and in Zimbabwe the population is of two distinct tribes. South Africa is multi-racial to the extent that there are nine separate ethnic and language groups within the one country: five black tribes, the Cape Coloureds, the Indians, and the two distinct groups of whites, the Afrikaans, and the English speaking. Certain black tribes are fierce enemies even to this day and tribal warfare still rages even within the civilisation of a major city like Johannesburg.'

It is almost assumed worldwide that the South African whites are all racist. This certainly is not true among the born-again, Spirit-filled Christians who are involved in this present reviving in South Africa. David Newington said, 'Emmanuel Press, based in South Africa, with a ministry to the whole of black Africa causes many questions to surface, and sometimes get voiced, like; "I thought all white South Africans hated blacks?"' David said, although their mail pours in from all over the world including on one occasion, twenty-seven African nations in one week, they rarely get any anti-South African attitudes being expressed.

Digging Out Racism

During all my travels in South Africa I only encountered one Christian in whom I detected a racist attitude and even he would have been horrified if he knew that it showed. The Spirit of God leads into all truth, and praise God he is educating and changing attitudes. One young man found himself deeply convicted about withholding the wages of the poor. The Lord challenged him to pay his house-servant a righteous wage, almost twice as much as the accustomed rate. Another young man told me in some detail how God had delivered him from an unconscious superior attitude towards other races. He'd grown up in a middle class Afrikaner family where his only close contact with black people was with the household servants. They were always affable but it never occurred to him that friendships and normal social relationships were possible between black and white.

During his time in university John was successful in securing a scholarship which gave him the opportunity of a year in an American university. This was the chance of a lifetime, his family were thrilled to see him go. When he arrived in Washington he was met by a group who host foreign students during their stay in the United States. The person assigned to especially care for him was a tall young black American. In a friendly, open, perfectly well-adjusted manner he welcomed the white South African and took him home to meet his family and then introduced him to his landlady, a big black woman, where John was to stay. John said the emotional shock set him reeling, he couldn't begin to think how he was going to manage. His whole past experience mitigated against him finding a way to make normal, friendly relationships. John, a young Christian who'd been baptised in the Holy Spirit, was very willing to be taught by God in this new situation. He began to relax, enjoy his studies, and experiment with the new exciting relationships.

John said, 'In the past, the first thing I used to notice about a person, was his colour. I had grown up with preconditioned responses according to what I saw. My year in the United States became a period of total re-education. Joe was the best friend in the world to me. He became a person, not a type; unknowingly he taught me so much. It may sound amazing to you, but I discovered that behind black faces were precious people who could be known, enjoyed, appreciated, just as much as anybody else:

but more than that, they were equally precious to God.' John was sitting next to me in the car as we sped towards Johannesburg. Turning to me he said, 'You must find this so hard to understand, but my mind had been conditioned. That year away made me a new person, but it hasn't changed the situation here.'

When the time had come for John to return again to South Africa, with his studies completed, he took a job and lived again in his parents home. He tried to tell them about his experiences in the USA but somehow they couldn't understand, and that world seemed so unrelated to John's present life.

The following year Joe had the opportunity to leave the United States and make his first visit abroad. He landed at Johannesburg airport. John met him from the flight. Suitable accommodation had been found for him where John would visit.

'I had so changed, Joe was a friend, someone I enjoyed and not a black man. I wanted my family to meet him and thought they would see what I could see, but I realise I made a great mistake. Joe came home with me and I treated him like any other friend. He sat and talked and ate with us, but I was creating a huge problem. My parents didn't know how to relate to him, felt awkward and suddenly very vulnerable. But more than that, the servants also couldn't cope with serving a black man at the table and see him sitting in the lounge as one of us.' John was most careful to speak highly of his parents. They own land near to Durban; at present many Indians in the area are unemployed, and out of genuine concern for these men and their families, his father is establishing light industry to help the poor become self sufficient. John will join him in the task. The complexity of the problem defies solution, only the justice and peace of the kingdom of God can answer South Africa's needs.

Evangelising Black Africa

The touches of revival among the white South Africans are widely published, but actually the movement among the blacks is equally momentous. Probably ten times as many blacks are getting saved than whites. Peter Pretorious, an evangelist with his wife Ann, founded Jesus Alive Ministries in 1983. By tent evangelism they take the gospel to the blacks. Peter said, 'I find in my ministry ten-fold more signs and wonders among the blacks. Their faith is simple. They're prepared to accept truth as it's preached. Africans grow up with the supernatural: spirit powers are part of normal life, but unfortunately those who find Christ often stay only one step out of the kingdom of darkness. Their churches are poorly organised, the Christians are not adequately taught the truth and have little discernment between spiritual powers.' Peter Pretorious said, 'The African church has an acute need for teachers and teaching material to release Christians into the life of the Holy Spirit, founded upon the word of God. On the positive side, black churches are generally more lively, open and extrovert in their ways of worship.'

Ann said, 'The work has been born at a time when there is a desperate need for more effective evangelism. God is at work, South Africa is experiencing revival. People's hearts are open in a way they've never been before. We need more evangelists who can gather the massive waiting harvest.' Peter went on to say, 'In the past when evangelists held meetings they had to believe that God would give them fruit for their labours, but today, it's changed. The people come running.' Peter added, 'For the last ten years God has graciously blessed the ministry of the evangelist but what is happening now is beyond anyone's expectations. We are used to the desperately needy coming to Jesus, but today God's mercy reaches even the wealthy, and those in high places. We now have four cabinet ministers saved. For a number of years we have been producing conditions for revival in this country, by actively doing the things that call down God's power and blessing. Now we are seeing the rising tide of revival, the fruit of evangelising and prayer.'

Peter said, 'There has been a repeated prophecy that God

would send the wind of his Spirit from the South. I'm not a bit surprised about the fantastic blessing of Bonnke's Cape Town Crusade. I'm sure it's part of the fulfilment of this prophecy. God is beginning a great reviving throughout the whole land. It won't take place without many difficulties and massive spiritual opposition but we are ready to see the victory in Jesus.'

As I talked with those directly involved in Christian work amongst the black Africans, they were acutely aware of the massive spiritual battle that is taking place for the nation. Repeatedly I heard the sentiment, 'We're not concerned for the politics, but we want to see the kingdom of God come.' Repeatedly it was agreed that the recent resurgence of rioting and political unrest is motivated by a direct counter-offensive in the heavenlies, against the tide of the Holy Spirit. The demonic powers are getting worried.

There are at least ten powerfully anointed evangelists working mainly in black areas. In the past the black church has lived on hand-outs from the white world but now, new black indigenous churches are teaching giving and expect their people to support the pastors and general evangelism. A lot of education is needed in this area, even to the whites who have a paternal attitude towards their black brothers.

Many white churches support a black mission work in homelands and townships. One pastor of a small white assembly said to me, 'The black work is growing fast, we have now baptised 200 people in just nine months. We support the pastor from our own church funds giving him a salary which puts him ahead of all his people.' When he noticed my questioning look he added, 'The blacks have an odd attitude: they only respect people who have money and are successful. To ensure the pastor is honoured among the people, we give him a good wage.'

As God begins to move by his Spirit through South Africa, money is being released from the pockets of the white church to fund evangelism and church planting among the blacks. Within a period of five months, support from within Africa for Reinhard Bonnke's evangelistic work has jumped from five to fifty-five per cent of the total budget, mainly due to gifts from certain big churches.

There are very few large churches among the blacks, except a cult movement called the 'Zionist' church, which is mixed up with traditional black magic and tribal cults. Annually about one million adherents gather in Pietersburg where they have blood sacrifice.

Despite this massive deception, the true church is growing fast, but mostly gathered in small groups of about 140 people. The churches split and divide to such an extent that there are hundreds and hundreds of different denominations, with hardly enough titles left to name a new one! Why should this be? The black churches struggle with the problem of chieftainship and domain. The Bantu are fiercely independent and so constantly split and divide. Someone has said, 'They are the freest people on the face of the earth, never coming under anybody's rule or control, each one marks out his own domain.' As you can imagine that kind of atmosphere doesn't make for unity. The black churches will co-operate together outwardly, but there is no true spirit of unity among them. Some of the splits and divisions, fortunately tend to further the work of God. Recently a huge split in a well-known denomination has brought about the birth of 240 new churches, founded by those who left! The late king of Swaziland, when asked whether he understood white South Africans said, 'Oh yes, I understand them perfectly well, they're just like us, each man wants to have his own little kingdom.'

'We've talked about the vision of trees and bushes,' Peter Pretorious said, 'the bushes are so important. We need many, many more. Big trees – yes, but they cannot cover the ground; masses of churches are needed throughout our black population as senders of light and truth. Somehow we have got to teach the churches. In the past 'maturity' has often brought a waning in spiritual fervour, I suppose this is because the teaching only produced head-knowledge rather than spirit and life. We want to be able to bring the right kind of teaching which will liberate gifts, produce ministries and increase evangelism.

The black African is a very humble person, open and willing, ready to accept the gospel. Talking to the blacks is so different to ministry among the whites. In South Africa the whites are carefully taught against supernatural manifestations, for fear of being infected by spiritism and the occult practices of the blacks. Our western civilisation has trained us to always look for natural explanations. Our motivations are so different. Peter said, 'You only have to tell Africans the truth and they receive it.'

Love Shed Abroad

Peter Pretorious, whose name advertises that he is an Afrikaner, told me an interesting testimony of how the Lord brought him to have a genuine love for black people.

At a time in his life when he was hungry for God and seeking guidance for his future, he felt the Lord led him to attend a certain conference. When he arrived, he discovered that he was the only white person registered. Peter found himself squashed in the small hall with 500 black pastors; his brothers in Christ. The stale smell of sweaty bodies filled the air. Peter was suffering culture shock, but his hunger for God caused him to put all the outward influences away and receive the word of God.

The invited preacher was an Assemblies of God pastor, a renowned black man called Elijah, who is mighty in the word of God. Reinhard Bonnke then followed brother Elijah. As the meeting closed, Peter stood in response to the word – the power of God fell upon the people, in a spontaneous act. Along with hundreds of black pastors and their wives, he was slain in the Spirit and buried under heaps of bodies. There didn't seem to be a square inch of floor left. He lay there abandoned to the Holy Spirit and unable to move. Eventually he attempted to stand up, as a very large black woman managed to trace her way through the bodies and stood before him. Peter said he felt surgings of love for all the people around him, his heart burned with love for them. The woman standing before him was evidently in desperate need. Peter put his arm on her shoulder and began to pray for her, his heart overwhelmed with love: from that day onwards it has never ceased. His consuming passion is to see Black Africa saved.

12: Green Valley

I was privileged to visit a man called Benjamin Solinda, who lives at Acornhoek, a black homeland in the Northern Transvaal. There had been very little traffic on the well-made road which took me through small scattered villages, across ranges of undulating hills and stretches of nondescript landscape. Often I passed groups of people with children walking along the roadside. There was no obvious place where they were coming from, or where they were going to, but as I drove past they greeted me with friendly shouts, waves and smiles. Enthusiastic youngsters would jump up from the shadow by the side of the road, armed with the choicest avocado pears, which they would hold up invitingly. The fruit of the fields was on sale all along the way. Grapes, oranges, sugar cane and at every stop—avocado pears.

A sign on the road announced Acornhoek and I began to look for the Green Valley furniture stores, my landmark where I would find Pastor Benjamin Solinda. In front of a large building announcing Green Valley Supermarket, many people were milling around in a dusty area by some petrol pumps. I turned the car towards the buildings and drove across the open dusty ground. People seemed to be more important here than cars, there was no clearly marked road. I tucked the car into a convenient parking place, got out and had a good stretch. The sun was warm, it was a lovely day, but more than that, there seemed to be a marvellous atmosphere around the Green Valley Supermarket. The place was as busy as a beehive, everybody singing, whistling, smiling, chatting in a most friendly manner and over all the hubbub, gospel choruses sounded out from loud speakers.

I asked some workmen on a building site where I'd find Pastor Solinda and surprisingly they directed me to go in to the supermarket. I waited a few moments and a small neat African man, in a well-worn pin-striped suit came down the back stairs to greet me. The whole complex of business and buildings appeared to belong to him, apparently organised as a complete Christian community under his direction. We walked round to the front of the supermarket, a rather grand name for a very remarkable shop. It's stock was somewhat unfamiliar to western eyes, with everything from farm implements, building materials, food, clothing, shoes and pretty little bone china tea sets. Besides these more easily recognisable items, many objects I couldn't identify. We passed through the shop and up the steps at the end to a mezzanine floor, where he had his office. From this tiny room overlooking the activities in the shop below, Benjamin Solinda organises all his business affairs, which are part of the spiritual ministry of Green Valley. I followed him into his office past a neat-looking Muslim salesman, sitting on a bench waiting hopefully to do business.

Preach, Preach, Preach!

In 1971 Benjamin Solinda started to build a church. He said, 'Even before that date I was preaching. We had gathered a number of people and the church became part of the Nazarene Mission, but in 1977 something happened to alter the whole course of events.' At four a.m. one September night in 1977, he was wakened from his sleep by the Holy Spirit who said to him, 'Preach, preach'. The Lord kept repeating the command till Benjamin said, 'Lord there isn't anybody here to preach to.' The Lord said to him, 'I want you to tell me that you will preach.' So he found himself telling God, 'I will preach, I will preach, I'll preach every day.' He continued telling the Lord over and over again,

'I'll preach every day, I'll preach every day.' The Lord said to him, 'You're not to pray, asking for things, you are to pray, agreeing with me. What I say to you, agree with me in prayer, agree now that you will preach.' That encounter with God revolutionised Benjamin Solinda's life. He has preached every day since then!

The same morning at seven a.m., he went to open up the supermarket as usual, to let the workers inside. He said to them, you go in but I'm going to stay here. The Holy Spirit had told him to preach outside the shop, so he stood there until sunset preaching to anybody and everybody who came past. At that time the shop was only small and Acornhoek is anything but a metropolis. Probably most of the citizens of that small community would have passed by at some time during the day.

That same evening a small prayer group gathered. Suddenly the Holy Spirit came powerfully among them in an unusual way, he seemed so close. Then as they were praying many demons began to be manifested. The front line of spiritual warfare was drawn in the small room where they gathered for prayer. Benjamin Solinda tried until twelve o'clock at night to cast the demons out, but with very little effect. He said, 'They were in the people who had come for prayer, the sincere ones who were seeking God.' He said, 'Most of them were Christians, some were not. The first thing that happened when the Spirit of God came was – we discovered demons. I was amazed at how many demons were at work among the people of God.

'The next day I preached and again I came in direct confrontation with demons. The Holy Spirit said to me, "If you want to chase these demons away you are going to have to fast and pray." We didn't know much about this, we had never done it before. After my encounter with God two nights earlier, I agreed with everything he said. If the demons were not going to go without us fasting and praying, I told God, "Yes, we will fast and pray." We went without food until ten o'clock at night and prayed that whole day. Immediately we had success. The demons went out of the people, many of whom were sick and they were healed. You see a number of the people in the prayer groups had come because they were ill and we found that as the demons went, they were healed. You can imagine, there was fantastic joy, those delivered from demons and healed from many sicknesses went everywhere testifying and preaching. Their witness brought more and more people. Crowds came with their sicknesses and their demons. Day in and day out, healings continued as we obeyed the Spirit of God. It is awesome, God only told me one thing, to agree with him and preach. He sent his Spirit and showed me the demons in the people. As they were driven out, the gospel went everywhere with power.

'Since 1971 we have had a church here. It had been a good church, but nothing outstanding. Its life was sapped by the stranglehold of demon powers, subtly and unobtrusively they held the work in smallness and ordinariness. Our experience of God was not his power but knowledge about him, which had saved a few.'

When all these things happened, Benjamin Solinda was officially a Pastor with the Nazarene Mission, although involved in his own business. As he continued preaching every day the momentum of spiritual activity rapidly increased. They purchased a tent and started a crusade ministry to the villages round about. Everywhere they went, people were being saved. It was like a miniature revival taking place. Obedience and preaching brought down the power of the Spirit. His activity exposed the presence of demons; much land has been taken in the spirit realm.

When spirits were manifested through the ministry of Jesus, the religious did not approve. Likewise the officials of the denomination deemed the happenings at Acornhoek unconstitutional, not according to their code of conduct. They insisted Pastor Solinda should stop preaching or resign from the mission. He couldn't comply. Painfully he accepted it wasn't men or demons driving him out, it was God, 'He chased us out to free us for a better thing. During that painful time I remembered a missionary lady who had visited us from Swaziland, some years earlier. She had prophesied that God would send revival to this place; a true prophet, her word came to pass through pain and difficulties.'

Heal the Sick

'We have many evangelists and preachers now, reaching out in a very wide area. Using the tent we preach and pray for the sick, and churches have been planted in the villages round about. There is no end to the opportunities, so we have recently bought a brand new tent costing 37,000 Rand.'

In between telling me this fascinating story Benjamin Solinda, the manager of the supermarket, was continuously interrupted by telephone calls, and requests from his staff. He's an amazing man, efficiently running a large commercial organisation, which provides employment for Christians in the area, as well as financially undergirding an extensive Christian work.

We left the office by the back stairs as Pastor Solinda wanted to show me the church buildings and hostels for the sick. As we walked he explained, 'Some of the sick require care over prolonged periods. We have now constructed two hostels, one for men and one for women. Those who are not immediately healed in meetings and who have incurable diseases can stay in a hostel with a person looking after them. We do not provide any medicine but through teaching and prayer they are healed.'

I put my head inside the door of the women's hostel where there were rows of beds and relatives moving around caring for the sick. The long room provided only the absolute basic requirements for living. It looked like a primitive hospital ward, although the building was brand new and clean. A very unnatural looking child, possibly mentally deranged, came towards me with her mother. The desperate condition of her daughter, had written deep lines upon her face.

I went outside again and Pastor Solinda pointed to an elderly lady walking across the courtyard. 'She helps to prepare food for the sick and dying.' As she drew water from the well, he said to me, 'See that woman, when she came she was carried in and had been bed-ridden for many, many years. Notice she still walks with a stoop, the healing's not complete yet, but we give thanks for the miracle so far.' Her condition was identical to the woman in the Bible, who had a spirit of infirmity for eighteen years, which bent her over so she couldn't straighten herself. I watched as the small black woman carried the bucket of water; the impossible is happening: little by little her back is becoming straight.

Benjamin Solinda said, 'We have people here in these hostels who come directly to us from the town hospital. Some are in urgent need of operations but they prefer to come here and get healed.' I asked, 'What do you do for them?' 'Their only medicine is prayer and the word of God. At seven a.m., as many as are able come to the supermarket for our prayer time. We meet from seven till eight each day. Then at ten a.m. in the hostels we teach all the people what the word of God says about healing. We bring them to faith and salvation, then again spend time in prayer. It's like four-hourly medicine, at seven, ten, two and again at seven, we teach the people and spend time with them in prayer. By hearing the word of God they get healed. The dying become perfectly well, cancers disappear, hopeless cripples are straightened, the mad and deranged come to their right mind.'

Prosperity and Hard Work

Looking about me I could see that the whole work demanded a phenomenal amount of personal care. I wondered how many pastors were fully involved in this ministry. Benjamin said, 'Many of those who were sick and at one time in these hostels, are now our pastors. As the work gets bigger and bigger so the number of workers is increasing. Some of our people have gone to Bible school, but we don't have any rules or regulations about these things.' I asked him how the work was financed. Was everybody involved in 'tent making' the same as himself?

'At one time I had a good carpenter who was also a very good preacher. For some time he did both jobs but felt God wanted to separate him to the ministry. I accept that God does that for some people, others here are involved in a variety of work. Yes, we support the whole mission ourselves. Our people are poor blacks living in this homeland area, but God has prospered them and they know how to give.'

We then walked into the church building. A brand new, lovely construction which they have built brick by brick themselves. It seats about 800 people and in this small community it is full each Sunday. Alongside was a building providing basic accommodation for the many pastors and their families. These are the men who stay to help the sick and suffering and preach in the district round about. As I walked through the building Pastor Solinda introduced me to different people and each time I was given their testimony. Again and again they had stories of outstanding miracles to tell. Many of these servants of God were people who had been brought back from the brink of death by a miraculous intervention.

The Nazarene Revival Mission and Pastor Benjamin Solinda may not be known to many people but they've made their presence felt to the powers of darkness. Almost by hand to hand combat with demonic forces they have rescued thousands of people and brought them into the kingdom of God. Pastor Benjamin's vision is huge. He longs for much, much bigger things, but he is also a wise man, he says, 'As we move forward I've got to be able to cope with all that God gives to me. I must only be involved with what I can truly look after. Others will work to fulfil the whole vision.'

13: Learning the Lessons

Throughout this book I have recounted what I have seen – what Christians are doing in a situation where God's Spirit is moving with far greater freedom than in most places. It serves us well to learn from those who at present experience what we long for. If by doing what they do, it could bring revival upon our own nation, that would be glorious; but in the spiritual realm, it is not that easy. The eternal paradox raises its head – what comes first, the chicken or the egg? Or in this matter – do we wait for God, or is God waiting for us?

God's Time

1979 was a significant year in South Africa. Many major churches were founded, and men with unusually anointed ministries appeared on the scene. Surely it is not a coincidence that in the year 1979 Nicky van der Westhuizen, Ray McCauley, Fred Roberts, Theo Wolmarans, to name but a few, began their churches. This prompted me to ask some questions. What happened in 1979? Satan didn't take a holiday! So what caused the breakthrough in the heavenlies?

Every new thrust of the kingdom of God and every new visitation of the Spirit is contested by the powers of darkness; they are militantly arrayed against God's purposes. His plans, though sure, are never implemented without a fight. The powers of darkness fight tooth and nail, desperate to hold on to their illegal territory as the believers come against them, armed with victory. Through faith, dogged determination – what the Bible calls steadfastness, the kingdom of God is established.

We shall never know who broke through the enemy and drove him out in 1979, but I am aware of a few who prayed and fasted, even forty days. God who sees in secret knows every one and acknowledges humble saints who have given him no rest, day or night; they have their reward. God answers prayer, giving the victory and the glory to Jesus.

Frequently I was told, 'Oh! It's God's time for South Africa.' Well what makes it God's time? Can we not fulfil certain injunctions and prepare ourselves for God's time? Yes surely! The Bible says, 'I will pour water upon him that is thirsty and floods upon the dry ground.' If we humble ourselves and seek his face, God has promised to heal our land. We can qualify ourselves for God's blessing.

Unknown saints, through their prayers, brought chaos and havoc in the ranks of the enemy, causing him to retreat in disarray. The victory is so glorious, that the church can now push forward its frontiers on every side, charged with new revelation and power. The same can happen again and again – and why not here? Perhaps God's time is when we wake up.

Knocking in the Wedge

A breakthrough is one thing, but a movement is another. What began in 1979 was glorious, but everything birthed in God grows, his work always tends to increase, but it doesn't happen automatically. The same spiritual energy that initiated, is required for its continuation. The mobilisation of prayer power across South Africa has broadened the whole front upon which the warfare is joined. On all sides the powers of darkness are under attack – the strong man is being robbed of his goods. Every demonstration of the power of God, every person healed, saved, or delivered is a further defeat for the principalities and powers who rule. Where once they exercised their power unchallenged, now they are retreating. Hallelujah!

The church that refuses warfare, that fails to mobilise its

strength to fight, will have little problem with the devil! Subtlety and deception are his ways. By small steps he eases the church towards the world, with such plausible reasons. 'Shouldn't the church be accepted in society, as one of the voices that speaks for the underprivileged or other social concerns?' When the cry of the church is drowned by political mimicry the church has lost its influence and has become little more than a welfare service. Before long, with minds squeezed into the world's mould, they question if there even is a devil! We are called to a spiritual battle, with spiritual weapons; the kingdom we work to establish is not of this world, said Jesus.

In South Africa the mighty band of intercessors have recognised the true reality of the spiritual forces arrayed against the nation. They have seen the enemy, taken stock of their resources, and deemed themselves able through God to pull down the strongholds. The war is against principalities and demonic forces, who want to keep people enslaved to wicked unseen powers.

Every significant movement of the Holy Spirit comes under attack, the automatic strategy of the evil one. Personalities are vilified, teaching is misrepresented, the devil will stop at nothing to discredit the work of God. History shows that too frequently a war or general political upheaval and disturbance, follows hard upon a visitation of the Spirit. It is not designed by God to test the saints as some would believe, but brewed in hell to frustrate the purpose of God and put a stop to souls being saved.

During the period of writing this book South Africa has continuously been in the news. Racial conflict, barbaric cruelty and hatred have made headlines day after day. Satan is rallying his forces, to impede the onward assault upon his kingdom.

Jesus is the only answer to the fantastically complex political jungle of South Africa. As the Spirit begins to gather momentum bringing the only possible solution to the nation's chronic pain, Satan has rushed in stirring up fresh militancy and chaos. Injustice is the ground on which he stands; he knows that as the Spirit surges forward his legitimate territory is being robbed from beneath his feet. The battle line is drawn, every conceivable effort is being made to stop the power of Jesus liberating South Africans into the family of God. The intercessors are alert, they are not ignorant of the devil's devices, and countless faithful pray-ers cry to God for their government, for wisdom, just reform, and peace to proclaim the gospel.

Many Christians will be amazed to think that God is pouring out his Spirit in South Africa – 'The society is unjust, it cries out for reform. How can God bless them?' I take comfort in the mercy of God. South Africa deserves nothing, but God has decided to bless, as he did in Nineveh of old. More than that, except God sends revival power upon South Africa, they have no hope. Only he can change men's hearts, replace hatred with love, superiority and disdain with humility, and injustice with justice. The blessing of God is the answer to South Africa's problems, which naturally are impossible to unravel.

Government, politicians and freedom fighters all have their solutions, none of which is guaranteed any success, because the changes called for demand new hearts and attitudes. Legislation doesn't change men, it changes laws.

In 1955 the Indian Government made it illegal to discriminate against the 'untouchables': yet nearly thirty years later, although they are now called 'harijans', sons of god, discrimination still lives on. The law is changed but caste is written in heart attitude, in high and low caste alike.

A second reason why I take comfort in God's mercy upon South Africa is that it encourages me to have faith that nowhere is too hard for the Lord. South Africa's complex politics and national injustice has not hardened God's heart towards them. His ear has been attentive to the intercessors. God hears prayer even for the most hopeless and desperate situations. As I look upon backslidden Britain, now renowned for its rebellion instead of its integrity, I take courage. God hears our prayer – nothing is too hard for the Lord. Those who pray, give the Lord no rest, persist, come again and again, we too shall see victory, God is full of mercy and long suffering – who knows whether he will not turn and pour out a blessing too vast to contain.

The Strength of Unity

Is unity a factor in revival? Is it an essential ingredient in preparing the way for the Holy Spirit to come in power? Frequently the subject came up in conversation, like a recurring theme. When Christians co-operate there is always a special blessing, but when the leaders come together in true unity in the Spirit, there is no limit to what God will do.

For Ed Roebert, coming together with other leaders became part of God's specific direction for his ministry. Seeking to fulfil the vision God gave him, brought him into contact with a number of influential men. Ed had no idea of the importance of those intitial encounters, or that God had an on-going purpose in them.

'Every man who does something for God has direction given to him by God.' The direction of Ed Roebert's ministry changed by reading an article with that title, written by Ralph Mahaney. It made him sit up and think – had he received direction? Did he know where he was going? Abraham did. Joseph did; God told him what was to happen. The anointed David knew he would be king. Ed had no such clear guidance, in fact, he wondered where he was going.

'Lord what would you have me to do?' He had to know, so he set himself to seek the Lord. Two things became clear. God confirmed a call to the city of Pretoria and to the country. What did this mean and how was it to be worked out?

Almost frustrated by his own smallness, he said to the church, the following Sunday, 'I would rather preach in a tent to twice as many people, than stay in this comfortable church as we are!' Within weeks they were out of the church and into a tent – the expansion began. He knew he could never fulfil the vision for the city alone, so he sought to develop closer relationships with pastors in Pretoria. The vision began to unfold; a large, influential, Spirit-filled testimony to the saving power of Jesus, in the capital city of South Africa.

The vision for the country was more difficult, but that was not made an excuse to neglect it. Ed meant business with God. He began to contact leading men throughout the nation. He felt cautious of the 'faith men' yet recognised God's Spirit with them. Prayerfully contacts were made and as relationships developed six men began to meet for fellowship; Ray McCauley, Tim Salmon, Fred Roberts, Nicky van der Westhuizen, Reinhard Bonnke and Ed Roebert.

The first step in obeying God may seem small – like Abraham leaving Ur of the Chaldeans, but wrapped up in the initial obedience, were the far-reaching purposes of God, that all the families of the earth shall be blessed. The Psalmist says, God commands a blessing where brothers dwell together in unity. These men with their wives meet every other month for two days because the Lord has brought them together. Out of fantastic diversity they have found unity and God is commanding his blessing upon them. Who can know his ultimate purpose in ordaining this fellowship?

Each of these men have powerful ministries and in one sense they have no need of anyone, yet their times together are given priority in very busy schedules. Nicky said, 'Ed initiated our gathering and he is like a father to the group. Our purpose is fellowship and mutual encouragement. It's a miracle that we have come together, we are so different, but what a remarkable unity we have found.'

Unity in the Spirit has become a reality. These men do not expect to have total agreement on function or doctrine but each expressed their oneness and surprise at its depth – they have come from such varied backgrounds. 'Our unity flows out of the deepest respect for one another as men of God; we honour each other and recognise that each is following the particular way the Lord has personally led,' said Ray.

The blessing of the relationship has been the cross-pollination that has taken place. They assist one another by their strengths and in their weaknesses. Reinhard Bonnke is the only one who is not leading a church but has an extravagant mission to preach the gospel from Cape Town to Cairo. His vision is shared by them all, not just in words – they have encouraged their congregations to financially support his work. South African churches want to see Africa saved. This is their means of putting feet to a genuine missionary concern.

These men represent some of the big trees with far spreading influence. Hundreds of churches are related to them individually. Under the banner of the 'International Fellowship of Christian Churches' each small church receives the wisdom and security of the brothers' own relationship. The blessing of their unity runs down over the 'little bushes' in dozens of different ways.

Unlike many other relationships, where a hierarchy has been evolved, these men meet as peers, as brothers who need to fellowship with men of like calling and stature. This is their strength. The forum provides a necessary place where blessings, needs and future vision can be shared and where men of gift and equal calibre can seek the Lord together. Frequently they share the same platform, and at times, become a convenient collective target for opponents of the work of God!

A bi-monthly meeting of a group of peer brothers may appear to be an insignificant thing, and it would be, except these men have obeyed God. He planned to especially bless them in an unusual experience of unity, which must be causing consternation among the hordes of darkness!

Power Is Not an Optional Extra

Power is essential – an accepted fact in the South African church scene, where those who have it are the success stories: it can't be hidden and invariably becomes a point of contention. Expanding congregations, miraculous signs and wonders by the power of the Holy Spirit are there for all to see.

Despite our personal experience of church life, or preferences, the truth is still the same; we need power if we are to have any impact upon our world. It may be that our local church's experience of the power of God is better than most in our district – but that is not a sufficient argument. Jesus told his disciples to wait in Jerusalem until endued with power – heaven's prescription for the church. This is the means God devised to establish the church in glory and authority, its motivation and ability to do a God-like job on earth. Only as we adopt the standards and produce the same life as set out in the New Testament, can we hope to hear, 'Well done, good and faithful servant.'

In South Africa, established church life is being fundamentally challenged by the unquestionable power and presence of God evidenced in certain meetings. If God works miracles there, why not here? We all need to question ourselves in that vein, it's an excellent means of shaking the dry bones. We need provocation; honest questioning could herald a new lease of life. Reality comes to those who hunger and thirst.

None can escape the necessity for God to be seen in their meetings as well as believed. In the light of a Saviour who died for the whole world, we must not underestimate the necessity to proclaim the gospel with power. There is no substitute for the promised Holy Spirit. His miraculous gifts breaking out in the South African church are the means for bringing in the crowds. Can we do without them? May God cause the gifts of the Spirit to break forth among us with mighty power. Let us seek, till we find. What a wonder it will be when our gatherings are not only to reaffirm certain tenets we believe, but times when we experience God's power so that we all become equipped to do the works of Jesus!

They Know Their God and Do Exploits

What we know makes us what we are. One of the outstanding impressions I gained by visiting the churches was the confidence of those who were being used by the Lord. Not self-confidence, but an unswerving, indomitable certainty that they were sent to do the works of Jesus and that they were fully able. It sounds very presumptuous but actually it was the speaking of child-like faith. They have the audacity to take God's word literally, as if written to them personally, and then to step out and do it – like Peter walking on the water. Jesus said, 'Come' – he obeyed and was immediately doing a miracle. If Peter had thought about it, discussed it, or reasoned the thing through, he would never have walked on water. True, it is impossible. He obeyed the words of Jesus – and the impossible became possible.

The same principle has revolutionised the churches. Their simple belief in the word of God has carried them into realms of power. 'Greater is he that is in you than he that is in the world.' With the word of God in their hearts they stand boldly against demonic powers, they expect to cast out demons in his name. They know their authority in God, they are seated with him in heavenly places, all things are under their feet. What can stand against them?

'You shall heal the sick.' Luke 9:10. The word of God is received as a command, and a commissioning. If God's word says, 'You shall heal the sick,' it means exactly what it says. Nothing is lost by simply obeying. 'You shall heal the sick,' all right Lord, that means I will heal the sick! 'I can do all things through Christ who strengthens me.' This is not presumption, foolishness or näivety – but childlikeness, of which Jesus said, 'Such is the kingdom of heaven.'

If we are to do the same works and even greater works, as the Bible promises, we too must know the riches of our inheritance in Christ and the full extent of our power and authority in his name. We begin by stepping out on the water as Peter did and find, like him, that obedience to the word guarantees the power to do the word.

Permanent Occupation by the Kingdom of God

I am sorry to talk about demons again, but whether we believe in them or not, demons (or evil spirits, as they are also called) are very active. The spiritual warfare in which Christians are engaged is not a phoney war. Demonic attack is as real as any conflict on earth and even more devastating.

When God pours out his Holy Spirit upon any district or nation, the immediate consequence in the spiritual realm is warfare! The battle line is drawn on a thousand fronts as evil spirits feel the impact of the pure Holy Spirit in the lives of changed men and women. They are forced to retreat, but cunningly attempt by any means to again occupy their lost territory.

Paul said, 'We are not ignorant of his devices' – unfortunately many Christians are, with the result that after a wave of blessing, evil again reasserts itself. In South Africa much new territory has been won. Thousands have been brought into the kingdom of God, huge churches established, under the devil's nose. Hallelujah! In fact he can do nothing to stop the relentless onward march of the kingdom of God, whilst the believers believe and give him no place. Jesus is the victor – that is not just words; he has defeated the enemy and the enemy is not going to win now. The victory Jesus won is for eternity, it wasn't a round in a fight – no, Jesus won the fight!

Hatfield Baptist Church has grown and grown – there is no sign of it stopping. There have been battles on the way when at times it seemed the devil had the upper hand. By harassment, opposition, slander, and every conceivable dirty means, he sought to oppose, but he has had to retreat every time. All he can do is to stand by and watch Jesus the Victor, demonstrating his endless power.

How do the Christians bring the Victor, Jesus on to the front line? It's simple really – they believe the word of God. 'Greater is he that is in you than he that is in the world.' As they walk forward to take back from the enemy, people for whom Jesus has paid with his blood, they know, really know, the Victorious Deliverer walks in them. They have authority and power over all the works of the enemy. It is glorious to know that in this wicked world we are ambassadors of victory, peace and eternal life.

Intimately linked with believing the word of God, is the prayer of faith. There are no new fancy methods. What has been gained by prayer is kept by prayer. The demons can always think up a new line of attack and the church must be one jump ahead, praying down the grace and power of God to defeat the deceiver. The size, power and above all, faith of a praying multitude in South Africa is reaping results. The general level of spiritual life in the churches has risen, and those born into the kingdom of God find themselves presented with a zealous faith-filled example, which they speedily copy.

Part of the Christian's armour, listed in Ephesians chapter 6:15, are shoes. Feet covered with the preparation of the gospel of peace. Feet are for going places – for making us mobile, and this in particular speaks of a travelling, communicating, freely available gospel. Our feet are for transporting the gospel. Every time we put on our shoes we should contemplate the armour of God. Feet which run with the gospel are wearing armour. Those who fail to witness, fail to use their feet for their God-given purpose – they have left off part of their essential armour. No wonder the non-witnessing Christian stumbles and falls. The South African Church has become a witnessing church. Men in influential positions in government and business talk the gospel, not ashamed to be known as Christ's men. Every stratum of society is being influenced. People are unabashed – their gospel is good news.

In this atmosphere men and women who object to what they call 'spiritual bombardment', can be equally unabashed in their opposition. On one occasion, whilst flying between Cape Town and Johannesburg, comfortably seated and waiting for my evening meal, a conversation began with the businessman sitting on my right. Twenty-five years ago he emigrated from England but still retained many very British attitudes – one of them was his insensitivity to the gospel! As soon as I started to speak to him about Christian things he fiercely turned on me, 'Oh God, you're not one of those born again types!' I got the impression that the 'born again' types were beginning to get underneath his rhinoceros skin.

Church life, where the word of God is believed and acted upon; where faith-filled praying prevails, and believers witness, is destined for growth and blessing. Churches founded upon these principles push forward the frontiers of the kingdom of God.

Large Churches

There is no doubt that the size of the many large churches in South Africa is a significant influence in the growth of the whole church. When I was in South Korea at Full Gospel Central Church I appreciated how that amazing congregation, now almost topping the 500,000 mark, is a sign to the world. In South Africa, the large churches, although so very much smaller than Seoul's outstanding challenge, are a sign to the nation. The sheer power of numbers raises them up above the mediocrity of so much church life. The Lord reigns, his power is unabated, they declare it over troubled South Africa.

The large cities of our land cry out for large churches. A church of ten thousand in the centre of London may be like a drop in the ocean – but it couldn't be ignored. The world would take notice – perhaps even the media, but more than that, a company of praising, worshipping people, thousands and thousands of them, would send a shock wave through the hosts of wickedness. The ruling spirits over the city would begin to tremble and be forced to let their captives go free. The spiritual climate would change, and where once it seemed so hard to find a response to the gospel, sinners would repent.

Large congregations of Spirit-filled, holy people cannot fail to have a large impact. The beleaguered few scattered in so many churches are incapable of producing anything but a minor assault on the powers of darkness. It is like taking on the enemy with only a hand pistol, when the situation calls for a whole army of artillery.

Huge congregations are not necessarily synonymous with shallow Christianity. We need to put away our preconceived notions about the best size for our churches. God's heart is as big as the whole world – he hasn't fixed a limit on those he will save, or the size of our churches. The eternal excuse of 'having time to consolidate the work' must be thrown off and trampled underfoot. It's the devil's lie to hinder evangelism. Believers must be carefully grounded in the truth, new Christians taught, the needy cared for, without neglecting the commission to continuously evangelise – it is always the time.

Large churches do not just happen. They have to be planned and achieved step by step, through determination and hard work. A man who owns a business has one objective in view, to make money. He would measure his success by his profit. The church should have one aim, to bring as many people as possible into the kingdom of God. If you liken financial gain in business with new converts in the church, most of the church would be declared bankrupt. It has failed to achieve its purpose for being.

Once the goal is clear, thought out steps have to be taken, all aimed at achieving the objective. A large church will not be built in a small hall. That is the first obstacle for many. The large churches in South Africa have all had to make the uncomfortable decision to move the congregation from building to building – very unsettling and inconvenient but essential to growth. No church will grow, consolidate the new converts, and keep the established congregation together, unless space is provided. Everyone needs to be able to come to the meeting, find a seat, have room for their friends and see enough empty seats to challenge them to witness and bring the people in.

Eventually when the nomadic congregation has grown too large to move, most South African churches have erected a building to suit their own needs. The ever expanding seating needs at Full Gospel Church in Seoul have been met by a continuous building programme. Let's see what happens in South Africa. Will their buildings now limit the extent of their growth?

If large churches are to be established in this country, a revolution in attitudes is required. All the resources of heaven are available to build the church. First we need to start thinking big, educating ourselves and the congregations so that expectation changes; no longer should we be satisfied with smallness. We want to see 'much fruit' to glorify Jesus.

Those Who Dare to Obey

A factor in the mushrooming growth of churches in South Africa are the 'spiritual entrepreneurs', those who dare to obey the promptings of the Holy Spirit and go out alone to see what they can accomplish for God. The Bible Schools seem to produce a number of young men and women fired with the Spirit who have only one desire – to serve the Lord. Charged with an overdose of zeal they are off; some may collapse after a time, but plenty go on. This old-fashioned missionary fervour is somewhat unheard of in British churches today, but when the Spirit of God moves with power again in our land, who is going to be able to hold down the modern-day Spurgeons, McCheynes, Campbells or Catherine Booths?

Marion Rankin is a remarkable lady with guts. She got baptised in the Holy Spirit, power came upon her and she was off! Talking, witnessing, gathering the converts, encouraging, teaching – there was no stopping her – she had a natural way with people and an authority in God. Evangelism was closer than second nature to her. Long before she could reason things out there were so many converts a church had been born.

Her husband has a profitable fruit farm, where he grows some beautiful avocado pears. As much as his business allows, they are together in the work, although he is sure leading a church isn't his calling in life.

Marion, a sincere, single-minded individual told me a story which perfectly illustrates why God uses her in remarkable ways. When teaching the church about the power of God's word, she knew she had to demonstrate it.

One morning the family wakened early to leave for a ten-day holiday in Israel. As Marion swung her legs to the floor, she immediately recognised some old symptoms; the unmistakable feeling of a thrombosis in her leg. She sat on the edge of the bed contemplating the situation for a few moments, and then went to the bathroom. She didn't want to let anybody know that this problem had recurred: first, she didn't want to spoil the holiday, and secondly, knowing the power of God's word to heal, she felt the challenge in her spirit to receive the fruit of her faith. Sitting in the bathroom, she began to claim the word of God – by his stripes, she was healed. With ferocity she went against the powers of darkness, telling them that they were not going to rob her of the benefits of God's word; by the stripes of Jesus she was healed, she was going to be healed, she was going to receive that healing and walk in it. She declared, 'This is my round, I'm going to win this, the word of God must prevail.' She said, 'I'm not going to take any aspirins, I'm placing myself in God's hands and trusting him to heal me.'

With the last things pushed into the cases, the family were ready to leave for the airport. Constantly claiming God's word, Marion left for their holiday. Some of their time was spent at a conference where Marion praised the Lord and even endeavoured to dance with the rest of the congregation. All the time, the leg was becoming more and more painful, and swelled up like a balloon, but she just continued to claim the word of God. She said, 'I was determined to behave as if I were healed, because I believed God's word, which said, "By his wounds you have been healed."' (1 Pet. 2:24). For the same reason, she did not opt out of the tourist activities, but involved herself in everything, despite the pain. One day followed another, and there appeared to be no improvement.

After ten days they were on the plane, travelling back to South Africa, the holiday behind them. The journey from Johannesburg to White River, where they live, takes four hours by car. Without thinking, her husband who was quite tired, said, 'Would you like to drive for a while?' completely forgetting that she had a painful leg. She eased herself into the driving seat quite determined to do everything as normal, as if the leg were healed; she managed, despite the pain, to drive the car back to White River. That night she fell into bed exhausted, but at three a.m. was wide awake. The presence of the Lord filled the room. God had wakened her. She felt her leg; it had shrunk to a perfectly normal size, and was completely healed. It had taken ten days, but now she had her own personal proof that 'by his stripes she was healed'.

Pioneers have to be determined people, and quite ruthless towards themselves. Marion can now speak to those who want to be healed with a new authority. Nothing is too hard for the Lord. She has some marks of amazing leadership; she doesn't talk theory, but only those things which she does know.

By any means the church must return to simple faith in

the word of God. Tragically even the Bible believing section of the church, so often qualifies and rationalises the truth till it has lost its punch. 'But . . . , but, and if . . . , and surely it's not always that simple . . . ?' Our list of reasonings knows no end. Jesus used the word of God against the devil as the final authority, without question or apology: the devil fled. He still does when we use God's word like Reinhard Bonnke, who says, 'God's word in my mouth is the same as God's word in his mouth.' Hallelujah; let's believe it and we will have the same results.

This is the essence of faith: God's word, believed and spoken by his people who expect him to act as if he were speaking it out of his own lips. Jesus said, 'Will I find faith on the earth when I come?' This is his heart's desire: that his people should be filled with faith, without which it is impossible to please him.

South Africa is not only rich in gold dug from the mines but in faith that has been tried and tested like Marion's and proven to be more valuable than fine gold. How many are willing to respond to the gracious invitation of the risen Lord to come and buy gold, refined by fire that we may be rich? Rev. 3:18.

14: The Glory

When God comes in revival power, people are left speechless, barely able to describe what is happening among them. They say, 'God came.' His awesome presence sweeps majestically across congregations, falls like dew, or comes like a whirlwind. With only a glimpse of his mighty person, the glory of God is sensed with every possible feeling.

South Africa, to the amazement of the world, is experiencing waves of refreshing. The tide is not yet at full-flood, but the intensity and extent of the visitation is deepening and expanding. His glory fills their meetings, supernatural happenings defy all questioning and confound the sceptics. The tidal wave of revival is edging in on the land.

We are accustomed to the particular awe which comes upon a meeting, when there is a prophecy or a tongue with an interpretation – we sense God is in the place. The gifts of the Spirit invite the presence of God, they are like a gateway through which his power flows; but many things I observed in South Africa were beyond the 'normal' realm of gifts of the Holy Spirit.

During one meeting, while Ray McCauley was preaching, he happened to point at a man sitting near the front, who had recently been converted. As he pointed, he said, 'And you shall be baptised with the Holy Spirit.' No sooner than the words were spoken, the man crumpled up and fell to the floor as the power of the Holy Spirit came upon him. He lay there between the rows of chairs for the remaining part of the meeting. Simultaneously, another man who had been closely watching Ray while he was preaching, slumped upon the floor as the Holy Spirit fell upon him; he too remained there till the end of the meeting. Finally, when these men stood up, they were both baptised in the Holy Spirit and speaking in tongues.

When that kind of thing happens in a meeting – what can we say? It's God. Nobody can 'stage-manage' miraculous events. Those who look on are filled with amazement; those who preach, preach the same gospel and do the same things, but God is openly coming among them.

Isn't your heart filled with longing like mine, that God should visit us in the same manner? Wouldn't it be wonderful, if instead of endless hours of counselling and persuading rational unbelievers, the Spirit of God just fell upon them? There is no reason why it shouldn't happen here. God is waiting to pour out his Spirit and send a mighty revival.

On another occasion, during the Sunday morning meeting at Rhema Bible Church, a young man was passing the building, returning from playing squash. He heard the singing and wondered what was going on inside. Opening the door he put his head in and stood at the back of the meeting amazed to see a great crowd of people singing and praising. With his hands on his hips, standing in his shorts and T-shirt, he surveyed the scene. Little did he know, he had walked into the presence of God. Before the young man knew what had hit him, God reached out his hand and laid him on the floor, smitten by the power of God. He stayed there for the duration of the meeting. When Ray gave the invitation for those who wished to be saved, he was set on his feet and came to the front, a saved man and flooded by the Spirit. Strange? No, it's God. Everything is new when the Spirit of God comes.

Working Where He Works

What must we do to prepare the way for the Holy Spirit to come in revival power upon our nation? This book has concentrated upon the power, signs and wonders in the move of the Spirit in South Africa. This is deliberate, because they characterise the present wave of revival sweeping through many countries. It is what God is doing today. Twenty years ago it was tongues and prophecy. Those looking for the glory of God ran and received everything being poured out. Let's imitate them and receive what God is doing and giving today; trample on unbelief, cast off excuses, renew our minds in the word of God and learn how to be channels for God's power. Surely we live in the last days when God will pour out the latter rain; a mighty, overwhelming deluge of the Holy Spirit. It will be greater than any visitation in the past and will cause today's wonders to pale into insignificance against the glories of tomorrow. What God is accomplishing in South Africa he can do here and much more, if we too stir up our hearts to seek the Lord. What prevents us from pressing in to receive the same blessings?

Nothing hinders from God's side, but many things restrict from our side. If we wish to see God's power and experience his glory, we must come hungrily to him. Earnest seekers find.

Working Out the Promises

We must receive power. God wants to heal the sick through you and open your eyes to the authority you have over demons. With his power upon us we can do the works of Jesus, not as a rare occurrence, but in abundance. They are intended to be an integral part of the normal life of the church.

We need to return to the Scripture so that we come with a right expectation and faith to Jesus the Baptiser in the Holy Spirit. He said we shall be baptised with the Holy Spirit and *power*; John the Baptist said, Jesus would baptise us with fire. Where is the power? Where is the fire? So many are content with only speaking in tongues.

It is time to repent of our powerless ways and come in faith with open spirits to receive. Go where the power of God is being manifested, imbibe the atmosphere – let faith arise in your heart. God can do acts of power through you. This is not the day of a few star-turns, the anointing of God is upon the whole body. We have such treasure within, and glorious power upon us – let us learn how to release it into life's opportunities.

We must pray. Join with those who know how to pray – who have their prayers answered. Let the Spirit teach you. The ministry of prayer is not a shopping list of requests, but powerful warfare where we can expect even the mighty angels of heaven to come to our aid. We are locked in a battle for our nation, the victory is certain, the prophetic word is sure, but like Daniel of old, we cry to the God of heaven. Will you pray like you have never prayed before? A spirit of repentance must fall upon the church before it will sweep the nation. Let us humble ourselves before a holy God, with weeping and mourning and plead for mercy. Stand in the gap for those who are without God and without hope.

We must be childlike in faith. What poverty has come upon the church for its lack of faith! Through elevating knowledge and intellect above God's methods of spiritual advance, we have been robbed. Our legitimate power has been snatched away. What has been the church's remedy? To employ a few specialists, seek the world's expertise for spiritual ills, while the whole body of believers sink into passive watching of the few working.

If we are to prepare the way of the Lord for his power and glory we must come like little children, believing and receiving, trusting his word and boldly acting upon it.

If you plan to lead that kind of life, almost every day you will discover yourself in a new situation, doing things you have never done before, and without experience upon which to call. Do not fear. That is how we advance, exactly how little children grow up and become mature. Every day they attempt something new and are not dismayed when it doesn't work the first time. Be continuously like little children, never become a 'know-all'. Cultivate the thrill of putting your hand into the Lord's and walking with him in the life of faith.

We must evangelise and be bold. The Spirit of God fell upon the first disciples for this one thing – to make them witnesses. The church in recent decades has pulled garments of shame about itself and retreated, almost unconsciously embarrassed at its powerlessness. Boldness comes from the Spirit of God; he can transform the shy and timid into fearless witnesses. Seek to be filled more and more by the Spirit and you will find you have something to talk about. Jesus your Saviour will be so much more real. The wonder of your salvation will bubble out and you will be talking of Jesus almost automatically.

Yes, it will be easier to witness when thousands are being saved – today it's a different matter. Perhaps you are the only Christian in your place of work. Earn a pioneer's reward! Preach the gospel where no one else has been – you will receive a pioneer's anointing!

It requires two people to play on a see-saw. If you are waiting for the day of God's power before you will witness, perhaps you will wait for ever! Why not sit on your end of the see-saw – start witnessing and you will find the power of God is there and you will start swinging!

We must pray for the sick and cast out demons. These are not optional extras for those who like to do that sort of thing. Praying for the sick and casting out demons are fundamental to the proclaiming of the gospel. Jesus made it so, by the things he said. There is a first time for everything. If you have never prayed for the sick before or you think you don't have the gift, why not launch out and try? There can be no success without the first experiment. Every victory is a defeat for Satan and every attempt, whether successful or not, is an object lesson in faith.

Each believer has potential authority over demons. The

devil doesn't like you to know that. He prefers you to be frightened of him. He would rather you thought that casting out demons was only possible to a few special people. The Deliverer dwells in you; he has already defeated Satan with his hosts. The risen Christ has vested you with authority, to continue his works and establish his rule.

I said you have potential authority, because actual authority depends upon our faith and availability to the Spirit. No life cluttered with sin, worldly lusts or fear is freely available to the Holy Spirit: many Christians only become earnest about their sin when it inhibits their happiness; a more essential reason for being freed from sin, is to become available to do the Lord's will.

We must have a strategy for growth. The outpouring of the Holy Spirit will bring a vast number of people into the church. Now is the time to plan and re-educate the Christians who have grown up in smallness. Many think a couple of over-sized families is an acceptable number for a church and three hundred is big! When revival comes, no buildings will be large enough to hold the crowds – every record will be broken, every norm cast aside. We will become accustomed to counting in thousands.

Coming back to the see-saw illustration, it is pointless dreaming dreams of revival, with thousands being saved, unless we are prepared to sit on the see-saw and work for a bigger church now, pray for growth, train leaders and evangelise. Many congregations will need to become an actual pilgrim people – leaving comfortably-fitted buildings for larger premises which provoke and challenge the believers to evangelise. Don't allow yourselves the luxury of settling down and enjoying success; growth means continuous change, uprooting and discomfort. The church needs to be taught that this is the normal Christian life. The Holy Spirit will show how changes are to happen. As long as he is the author of the unsettling he will supply the necessary grace.

Once the decision is made – 'By God's grace, we are going to grow and bring forth much fruit to glorify Jesus' – wisdom and strength will flow and growth you never thought possible will begin to happen. Jesus wants you to grow. He is waiting for you to agree with him. Put the weight of your actual earnest intentions upon one side of the see-saw and watch. Whatever you put there will be matched by the power and ability of God.

We must hear and obey the Spirit. The hearing of most people diminishes with the progressive years. Strangely, the same is true of so many Christians. They begin life with perfect hearing, thrilled at being guided by the Lord, but even after a short space of time, it is possible to stop hearing – or does the Lord no longer speak? With those who hear and then obey, he continues to communicate. When the excitement of being directed by the Lord is tempered by a lack of willingness to do what he says, the voice of the Lord becomes rare.

Come let us return to the freshness of those days when we first heard the Lord speak. What a delight it was to realise every detail of our lives was being ordered by him. He gave instruction on the books we read, the music we listened to, the company we kept, the entertainment we enjoyed – what a personal relationship! The Lord wants to move us on from ordering our lives to directing our service: when to witness, when to miss out of 'fellowship' to be alone and pray, when to give, when to deny oneself, when to move in the gifts of the Spirit, when to be quiet. He will speak if you will listen – if you will obey.

How can we do God's will except we hear him speak? These are crucial days; let us train our ears to hear, so that we can effectively co-operate with the Spirit. We must motivate every believer. Let's not underestimate the size of the task. If the Spirit of God is to be poured out again in revival power we need to mobilise the whole church. Every member of the body has a vital function and must be put to work, each according to his or her gift.

If we follow these injunctions, we will build a great highway for our God – our actions will speak louder than our words or idle dreams. We will show our works so that he can see our faith – faith completed by works (Jas. 2:18, 22).

At the God-appointed time the King of Glory will walk down the prepared way and we shall be like the psalmist – like those who dream, our mouths will be filled with laughter, and our tongues with shouts of joy – the Lord has done great things for us, Hallelujah, we are so glad!

I am not day-dreaming, rather I am like Elisha's servant straining his eyes looking to see God's answer – those who believe shall not be put to shame. What God is doing in South Africa – and so much more – can be our portion. Through faith and patience let us inherit the promises.

If you wish to receive *regular information* about *new books*, please send your name and address to:

London Bible Warehouse
PO Box 123
Basingstoke
Hants RG23 7NL

Name ____

Address ____

____

____

____

I am especially interested in:

☐ Biographies
☐ Fiction
☐ Christian living
☐ Issue related books
☐ Academic books
☐ Bible study aids
☐ Children's books
☐ Music
☐ Other subjects

P.S. If you have ideas for new Christian Books or other products, please write to us too!

Other Marshall Pickering Paperbacks

THROUGH DAVID'S PSALMS

Derek Prince

Derek Prince, internationally known Bible teacher and scholar, draws on his understanding of the Hebrew language and culture, and a comprehensive knowledge of Scripture, to present 101 meditations from the Psalms. Each of these practical and enriching meditations is based on a specific passage and concludes with a faith response. They can be used either for personal meditation or for family devotions. They are intended for all those who want their lives enriched or who seek comfort and encouragement from the Scriptures.

LOVING GOD

Charles Colson

Loving God is the very purpose of the believer's life, the vocation for which he is made. However loving God is not easy and most people have given little real thought to what the greatest commandment really means.
Many books have been written on the individual subjects of repentence, Bible study, prayer, outreach, evangelism, holiness and other elements of the Christian life. In **Loving God**, Charles Colson draws all these elements together to look at the entire process of growing up as a Christian.
Combining vivid illustrations with straightforward exposition he shows how to live out the Christian faith in our daily lives. **Loving God** provides a real challenge to deeper commitment and points the way towards greater maturity.